2

D1381561

I243280

A 1950s Housewife

Other Books by Sheila Hardy

The Village School, Boydell Press/Anglia TV, 1979

1804 …That was the Year …, Brechinset, 1986

The Story of Anne Candler, SPA, 1988

The Diary of a Suffolk Farmer's Wife: 1854–69, Macmillan, 1992

Treason's Flame, Square One Publishing, 1995

Tattingstone: A Village and Its People, self-published, 2000

The House on the Hill: The Samford House of Industry 1764–1930,
self-published, 2001

Frances, Lady Nelson: The Life and Times of an Admirable Wife,
Spellmount, 2005

The Cretingham Murder, The History Press, 2008

Arsenic in the Dumplings: A Casebook of Suffolk Poisonings,
The History Press, 2010

The Real Mrs Beeton: The Story of Eliza Acton, The History Press, 2011

A 1950s Mother: Bringing up Baby, The History Press

A 1950s Housewife

MARRIAGE AND HOMEMAKING
IN THE 1950s

SHEILA HARDY

The
History
Press

To all the housewives of the 1950s, their daughters
and granddaughters.

First published 2012

The History Press
The Mill, Brimscombe Port
Stroud, Gloucestershire, GL5 2QG
www.thehistorypress.co.uk

British Library Cataloguing in Publication Data.
A catalogue record for this book is available from the British
Library.

ISBN 978 0 7524 6989 8

Typesetting and origination by The History Press
Printed in Great Britain

Contents

Acknowledgements

I owe a huge debt of gratitude to all those who, with great generosity, honesty and good humour, shared their memories and often their precious mementoes with me. So my thanks to: Mesdames Angland, Billsberry, Bolton, Brittain, Coker, Hale, Hepburn, Jacobs, Lankester, Lawrence, Lemon, Perrins, Porter, Randall, Richardson, Slater, Smith, Stannard, Titshall, Watkins and Wheeler. Thank you too, to the Troll family of Cumbria, Pamela Henderson in Wiltshire and Patricia Yelland in Suffolk; valuable contributions also came from the members of the Grundisburgh Lunch Club and the 55 Alive group at the Chantry Library in Ipswich. My sincere thanks too, to the men who became involved in my search: Gordon Bolton and David Bray provided some very useful photographs. David Burnett gave information about the Suffolk chlorophyll industry while John Kirkland happily allowed me to draw on his wide knowledge of the banking world as well as the magazine collection of his late wife, Monica. My sister-in-law Ursula Hardy loaned me a very precious and most helpful copy of *Woman's Weekly*, dating from 1959, while Rachel Field gave practical help and support. I am also indebted to the following representatives of the firms owning the copyright of some of the material used here: Emma Dally of Hearst Magazines, UK, for permission to include the Mince and Macaroni recipe from *Good Housekeeping's Popular Cookery*, David Abbott of IPC Media, Colin Raistrick of Proctor

& Gamble and Novia Imm of Hoover-Candy. Thank you, each and every one, but especially my loving and long-suffering husband, Michael, who unexpectedly found himself experiencing the life of a housewife during the writing of this book.

Author's Note on Illustrations

All the photographs and items of personal memorabilia herein have been reproduced with the permission of their owners, all of whom have been thanked in the Acknowledgements. However, in respecting those who wished for anonymity, it was decided that only descriptive captions should appear on each illustration.

Introduction

To someone who spends most of her time researching the lives of those who lived in the eighteenth and nineteenth centuries, the idea that the second half of the twentieth could be classed as history came as a shock. How could the 1950s, a decade from my own life, possibly be looked at in a historical context? I was suddenly confronted with having to heed my own teaching. I had so often cautioned my audiences to beware of sweeping statements and stereotypical pictures of, for example, the Victorian Age, reminding them that Britain in 1837 was a very different place to the country in 1901. How often have I had to hold my peace when a class of children announced they had 'done' the Victorians when in fact all their learning had been focused on a mixed bag of facts about the last twenty years of the reign.

Having recovered from the suggestion that I was now considered part of history, I began to see the advantages of writing about aspects of life in the 1950s. Doing the required research would at least give me a valid reason to bore my grandchildren with stories of what life was like 'when I was a girl'. In an effort to be as accurate as possible, I enlisted the aid of others and together we set out down memory lane, trying hard not to fall into the trap of talking about the good old days on the one hand and exaggerating how hard life was on the other. We ended up amazed at the changes we have witnessed – not all of them for the better – and we lamented some of the things we had lost, but also gave thanks for the many benefits we have gained. It has done us good to examine our lives in relation to those of our parents' and to look at where we fit into the social history of the twentieth century. I hope this book will be enjoyed by those who can say, 'Oh yes, I remember that!' as well as those who didn't listen, but now wish they had, to the stories their mothers and grandmothers told them. And to the young who may one day be studying the history of Britain during the reign of Elizabeth II, I offer just a small insight into the lives of young women who became housewives in the 1950s.

There are those who describe the Festival of Britain in 1951 as the defining line between the past and the present: where we turned our backs on all that was old and looked forward with optimism to everything new. It is true that this Great Exhibition was indeed a showcase for what the country could achieve and held out promises of the comforts that could be ours – sometime – in the future. My own view is that the real turning point came in the mid-1950s, after rationing ended and many of the restrictions that had affected so many different areas of life were finally lifted. Even in so short a period as ten years, there were such vast differences in how life was lived that it was impossible to say 'this is how it was in the Fifties'. And even to give a general view, it is necessary to look back to what helped to shape them.

The girls embarking on married life in the 1950s were products of the two or even three decades earlier. Their parents would have lived through the First World War, and it is likely that some of their fathers emerged from that with both physical and psychological injuries that would have affected their home life. The immediate post-war period of the 1920s is often depicted as a giddy, frivolous time – as it was for a certain class – but for the bulk of the population it was the era of great social unrest that, in the General Strike of 1926, highlighted the wide divide in the British class system. Of much greater impact was the period between 1929 and 1932, when the crash of the stock markets both here and in America had far-reaching economic effects, leading to what became known as the Depression. Unemployment was rife and home life for many was disrupted when fathers were forced to leave temporarily to seek work in other areas. This often left wives and mothers in desperate circumstances, scrimping to pay the rent to keep a roof over the heads of the family, as well as feed and clothe them all. Invariably, in an age when the only way out of a tight situation was to borrow money either by pawning items – father's best suit and mother's wedding ring being the most popular items – or from a loan company that charged high interest, it was not long before the family was forced to seek assistance from the Poor Law Board. Niggardly allowances were often handed out in such a manner that did nothing to help the recipients' 'feeling of self-worth' – a phrase and a concept unheard of at the time.

The 1930s continued to be a time of turmoil with the Abdication Crisis of 1936. Following the death of King George V at the beginning of the year, the Prince of Wales was formally declared his successor, to be known as Edward VIII. The prince had been tremendously popular with the working classes. They felt he understood and sympathised with their plight far better than any politician; to use a phrase, again unheard of at that time, he had charisma, which manifested itself when, for example, he visited striking miners in South Wales or the unemployed in the north. But, although there were rumours, the people knew little of the seriousness of his friendship with the American divorcee, Mrs Wallis Simpson. We had to wait until the twenty-first century and the development of internet channels before the private lives of celebrities became common knowledge. In the 1930s the press and cinema newsreel pictures were discreet, so it came as a shock to a large part of the nation when it became known that the new king wanted to marry Mrs Simpson. It was a shock because it struck at the heart of everything the monarchy stood for. Royalty was expected to marry royalty – a suitable princess from one of the European countries could be found – or, if not, at least a young woman from amongst the English aristocracy. The Church did not recognise the remarriage of a divorcee while the previous partner was still living. Thus, as head of the Church of England, the king could not marry someone who had had not one, but two, previous marriages. At a time when the barriers of class still predominated, the expectation of the majority of the population was that those in authority should set an example and, for most people, even those who did not marry in church, the expectation was that once married they would stay with their partner through thick or thin. When it became necessary for Mrs Simpson to obtain a divorce from Mr Simpson, she discreetly took up residence for a short time in the quiet east coast seaside town of Felixstowe (it was out of season), in the hope that her divorce suit might pass unnoticed when it was heard in court in nearby Ipswich. It was rumoured amongst the locals, after the event, that all off-duty policemen were required to fill all the seats in the court, including those normally reserved for the press. True or not, it was certain that children of the town quickly learned to sing:

Who's this walking down our street?
It's Mrs Simpson's bandy feet
She's been married twice before
Now she's knocking at Edward's door.

Not quite Facebook or Twitter but it spread just as quickly.

Before his Coronation could take place, Edward abdicated (an act almost unknown in British history) and his place was taken by his brother Albert who reigned as George VI and was the father of Queen Elizabeth II. Having survived that storm, and with the country gradually settling down to slow economic growth, outside pressures came with the rise of fascism, particularly on the Continent, with the increased power of Hitler and the Nazi Party in Germany, Mussolini in Italy and Franco in Spain. Many idealistic British socialists got their first taste of modern warfare when they went off to fight in the Spanish Civil War of 1938. Then, just four months before the fourth decade of the twentieth century began, Britain declared war on Germany.

Our 1950s bride was at that time coming towards the end of her school days. After six years at primary school, those whose parents could afford it sent their daughters either to a small school for young ladies (reputed to specialise in flower arranging and not much else) or to the fee-paying grammar schools for girls. These schools offered a proportion of free places each year to 11-year-olds who passed the Scholarship, an examination taken in two parts. The written papers were taken in the pupils' primary school but the oral part, which was taken only by those who had passed the written exams, took place at the grammar school. It lasted for most of the day, the candidates attending lessons, having lunch and finally enduring an interview with the headmistress. It was rumoured that this weeded out those with poor manners, particularly at the table! Once accepted, the girls and their classmates would have enjoyed an academic education leading to the School Certificate, taken at 16. Those girls who were considered clever and aspired to enter one of the professions – mainly teaching at this time – stayed on to take the Higher School Certificate. The option, apart from nursing, for those who left at 16 seemed to be mainly in secretarial work, so often a year followed learning shorthand and typing to the required speeds at either a Pitman's or private secretarial college. For the rest of the female population, in towns they progressed at 11 to central or municipal secondary schools where they had a watered-down version of the grammar school curriculum, but one that was preparing them for work in shops and offices when they left school at 14. In country areas, pupils might stay at the same school for their whole school career and the curriculum there was heavily biased to the idea that the girls coming from an agricultural background would continue in it after marriage. At least by this time domestic service was no longer the main career path for girls. Those with skills such as dressmaking were in demand in factories, while those entirely unskilled could still find work that suited them.

But then it all changed. The declaration of war in September 1939 brought major upheaval on many fronts and hurtled our future 1950s bride along unforeseen paths. Those still at school might have found themselves evacuated with their schools to different parts of the country. City girls found themselves among unfamiliar rural landscapes. Families were broken up and new ties, some very long lasting, were forged with strangers from very different walks of life. Career plans for some might have to be put on hold, while for others the war brought opportunities of which they had never dreamed. For many there was the option to join one of the women's branches of the army, navy or air force, bringing with it the opportunity to learn such skills as driving, mechanical engineering or plotting the movements of aircraft. Girls whose educational standard would previously have prevented them from becoming nurses, found that hospitals were happy to admit them as probationers, while older girls found themselves being 'directed' into war work in munitions factories, and into agriculture to replace those young male farm workers who had either enlisted or been called up for service. As more men were released to the services, so more young women began to do work that had once been the preserve of the male. The female 'clippie', as the replacement of the male bus conductor became known, was one thing, but there were those who thought it a step too far when a 'slip of a girl' was seen at the wheel of a double-decker trolley bus.

Alongside the great change in a girl's working life during the 1940s came the unexpected freedom of her social life. The pre-war girl would have met boys of her own age most probably from among her own social circle. The middle-class girl would have been a member of the tennis club and would have joined in all the other social functions that the club provided, while her less well-off friend would have relied on meeting a boyfriend either through work, a mutual friend or at the local dance hall. The parents of the pre-war girl would have probably known the family of any boy she met and would have been careful to vet their daughter's friends. But everything was different now. Girls who would have lived at home until their marriage were now often living miles away from parental supervision and many were having the time of their lives. Young men in uniform were very attractive, and in their off-duty time looked for female companionship. So it was that girls from the 1940s onwards found themselves future husbands from not only all over the United Kingdom but also from the United States, Canada, Australia and New Zealand as well as Europe – plain Miss Smith or Jones could have found herself becoming Mrs Unpronounceable.

So our 1950s brides entered the post-war period shaped by what had gone before. For the older ones, having had more freedom their horizons were much wider than those of their parents and their expectations of life were greater. The younger ones, in contrast, had been subjected to a much tighter discipline from home and school. It is said that theirs was the last generation to obey orders without question. Yet like the generations of women who had preceded them, they were about to take the biggest risk of their lives, that of committing themselves to becoming a wife and possibly a mother. We shall find out how some of them coped with this challenge.

1

Going Out

In the 1950s young men and women 'went out' together. Embarrassing uncles were likely to ask, in the sort of whisper that was audible to everyone else sitting round the Sunday tea table, if you were 'courting' yet. Auntie would look coy before saying she was sure it wouldn't be long before you found yourself a nice young man. Like as not, your mother, as she poured tea into the best china cups that came out of the glass cabinet only when you had visitors, as well as at Christmas and for funerals, would assert firmly that there was plenty of time for that sort of nonsense! And the company would all nod in agreement as they worked their way through a salad with ham or even a precious tin of red salmon, followed by pineapple chunks accompanied by a dollop of thick cream from a tin or evaporated milk (both decanted, of course, into a small glass bowl or a jug).

But was there time? For a girl in the 1950s there was still great pressure to find herself a husband. It was expected, or at least accepted, that she would find a 'nice' young man, marry in her early 20s, have children and be a grandmother by her mid-40s. Any young woman who reached the age of 30 without being married or engaged was regarded as being 'on the shelf', soon to be labelled as one of life's spinsters. And the mother who had been certain that there was plenty of time had to start finding excuses for her daughter's lack of matrimonial prospects. Onlookers wondered what was wrong with her: why didn't she catch a man like all her friends? The unattached female who could claim that she was far too busy pursuing a career was fortunate. That is, until her peers let her down by having a career and a husband!

So where did the 1950s girl find her man? In the early part of the decade single-sex secondary schools were the norm, certainly in towns. Traditionally, from the days of the introduction of compulsory education in 1870, the sexes had been taught in separate classes even if in the same building. There are still some very old school buildings in existence with entrances labelled 'Boys', 'Girls' and 'Mixed Infants', the last designation providing comedians with the opportunity for jokes. There were also different playgrounds for each group to make sure there was no fraternising during school hours. Even the 1930s wave of new buildings for grammar and senior schools tended to be just for one sex, frequently situated on sites at a distance from each other. In those cases where the Local Education Authority had restricted land available, the boys' and girls' schools might be on adjoining sites, in which case a sturdy high fence down the middle of the playing fields ensured that 'ne'er the twain shall meet'. But, of course, they did! Teenage boys and girls met as they made their way to and from school; the establishment might segregate the sexes but the local bus service didn't, and many a romance began at the bus stop. Boys soon got to know which routes, whether on foot or bicycle, were followed by the object of their interest. Once a friendship had begun, it was not long before the pair was deemed to be 'going out'.

'It will be a waste of time, she'll only get married' was often to be heard when discussing a schoolgirl's future.

The second most popular place for young people to meet was through attendance at church or chapel. During the 1940s most young children were sent to Sunday School as a matter of course and well-organised churches made sure that their young adolescents – teenagers was not a word in common use – did not drop their attendance by offering other activities during the week. A Bible class for example, a youth choir perhaps, or membership of the affiliated Scouts and Guides or the Nonconformist Boys' and Girls' Brigade.

How many young men wearing that neat little cap at a jaunty angle had set a girl's heart on fire as they marched to chapel through the streets on a Sunday morning, blowing a cornet or banging a drum? The biggest heart-throb, a handsome youth usually slightly older than the rest, marched at the front of the procession, carrying the silver-headed mace with which he performed such miracles of artistry as he tossed it, so nonchalantly, into the air. One had to admit that in the attraction stakes, the Boys' Brigade uniform beat the Scouts' hands down! So, romance often blossomed through the church and this, of course, was an advantage because the parents of the couple would already know each other, at least slightly, and the respective mothers could be content that their son or daughter was 'going out' with someone 'nice and respectable'. Ah, 'respectable', how often we heard that word in the 1950s!

In 1947 the school-leaving age was raised from 14 to 15 for most pupils. However, those in grammar schools were expected to stay until they were 16 in order to sit the School Certificate or Matric, as it was known. Their parents had to sign a bond, which carried a forfeit of £10 (more than a week's wages) if it was broken, agreeing to this extra year. Doing well in the exam meant you could leave and enter certain professions; alternatively it qualified you to enter the sixth form to study for the Higher School Certificate, which in turn could lead to university or college entry. There was a strong feeling among many parents at the time that it was most important for their sons to receive the very best education they could get, while many bright girls were denied the opportunity to stay on into the sixth form and go on further. 'It will be a waste of time, she'll only get married' was often to be heard when discussing a schoolgirl's future. So they, like the majority of the 15-year-olds from the senior schools that had now become secondary moderns, had to find a job.

Once she was out to work, then 1950s Miss was free to enjoy a social life. This was most likely to include dancing. During the wartime period of the 1940s dance halls had flourished throughout the country and had provided a pleasant and innocuous pastime for troops billeted away from home. Saturday night dances were held in village halls, school and church halls, right up to the commercially run Lyceums and Mecca ballrooms. Girls usually went with their best friend to enjoy the music and to practise the dance steps they had learned from other girls, usually during wet dinner hours at school, or at home from the wireless. Victor Sylvester, with his strict tempo dance orchestra, regularly broadcast an evening programme, during the course of which he would give instruction on how to perform a particular dance. Up and down the country girls would be stepping across the living room floor listening carefully to his well-known voice intoning, 'slow, slow, quick, quick, slow'. Some even got as far as the tango! But there was a problem. If you practised with your friend and you were taller than she was, then you got landed with taking the man's part. This could make for confusion when you got to a proper dance and a young man asked you to dance.

Once inside the hall, having paid the 1s entry fee, and the 3d to leave your coat in the cloakroom – a coloured ticket with a number on it was given as a receipt – the girls tended to sit or stand together while the young men congregated at the other end of the room, thus creating something of a male mini-stampede when the music started. This was the moment when some girls stared into space, hoping and praying that they wouldn't be left unpartnered, while the more blasé decided to be picky in their choice. Throughout the evening a live band played traditional ballroom dances, interspersed with the dreaded Paul Jones, supposed to be a bit of an icebreaker by mixing folk up, but a nightmare for some who were suddenly faced with Mr Flatfoot, Mr Toecrusher or worst of all Mr Breathe-down-your-ear as a partner. For the truly energetic – and if you were fortunate with your band – there would also be a chance to jive. This was something the girls could do as a pair; in fact, if there was a shortage of men willing to dance, it was quite usual for girls to dance together.

What everyone was really waiting for was the last waltz. This dance signalled the end of the evening and was the moment many young men had been waiting for. Having decided early on which young woman had caught his eye, he would make sure that he partnered her for the last waltz and, as the lights dimmed and they slowly circled the floor, he would ask if he could see her home. If she liked the look of him she would agree, if not then she would come up with an excuse to extricate herself. The chances were that she was in a dilemma because she had come with her friend who was still sitting with the other wallflowers. Should she remain loyal to her friend or take the nice young man's offer? If she accepted, then he and she would stroll leisurely back to her house and when they reached her front door he might suggest they meet again, perhaps to go to the pictures. With a chaste kiss, he would leave, just before her father or mother came to put out the milk bottles on the doorstep. And thus might begin another 'going out' that could eventually lead to marriage.

The workplace offered another popular way to meet one's future husband. From offices to factories to department stores, all with a large number of employees, it was easy to make friends with a colleague who might one day become one's husband. For some people a more preferable way of meeting a suitable soulmate was through a social function such as a friend's wedding, a cocktail party or a dance at the Young Farmers' Club, the tennis club or the youth wing of one of the political parties. A shared interest in politics, or a particular sport or hobby seemed sensible. From the parents' point of view this was much more satisfactory than having your daughter 'picked-up' by a stranger whom she met somewhere by chance. The man who had picked up her dropped glove in the library, the one who had talked to her in the park when she was out with the dog, the sailor who had asked his way to his ship, even the blind date arranged by a friend, all these were greeted with decided suspicion when they came to call for her and inevitably, should the romance progress, the young man would have to face the parental third degree when invited to a rather stiff Sunday tea. The prime concern of parents was that any future son-in-law should have a good steady job with at least the prospect of a decent income and so be in a position to provide their daughter with a comfortable home. If they were honest, most mothers hoped that their daughter would eventually settle near them, as they themselves had done – meaning that they would be on hand to help when necessary. But the war had changed that.

A great many girls fell in love with servicemen who came from different parts of the country, and who expected their wives eventually to go with them to their native area. We must not forget that there were still a great many servicemen around in the 1950s, as every able-bodied young man was expected to do two years of National Service in one of the three armed services. Those young men who had joined the Merchant Navy straight from school were exempt from National Service, provided they remained at sea for at least six years. They were expected to undertake certain training courses that would enable them to take part in defensive action should a national emergency arise. There were also still large numbers of American personnel in air bases all around the country. Most of the girls marrying them found that they would ultimately follow the GI brides of the late 1940s who had sailed the Atlantic to that vast continent, and discover for themselves that it was not necessarily the same as it appeared on the cinema screen. Other 1950s brides-to-be, particularly in the early years, found themselves facing life with an unpronounceable surname, when they married German or Italian former prisoners of war. These young women often had to face strong prejudice from both their families and neighbours. Post-war, many Polish ex-servicemen chose to remain in England, as did those from Hungary who were drafted in to undertake the very dangerous task of clearing mines from the beaches of Britain's coastal areas. Girls who married these men were not subjected to criticism, especially as often they had met them through social activities at the local Roman Catholic church. But it has to be said that there was a very strong colour prejudice in the 1950s. Girls who were brave enough to date a black American serviceman were often ostracised by their communities, never mind their parents, and matters did not improve when migrants from the Caribbean arrived. The hostility and hardship faced by these men and women has fortunately now been well documented.

So, our 1950s girl has been going out with her man for some time and at last he has plucked up the courage to ask her to marry him – or at least decided he loves her enough to want to spend the rest of his life with her. She has probably dropped enough hints that what she wants is marriage. To be brutally frank, in the 1950s that was the only way a couple were going to enjoy a fulfilling sex life. It is difficult to work out what was the average length of time that a couple knew each other before committing themselves to an engagement. Amongst my contributors the longest was seven years, while for sheer speed it is hard to beat the couple who met and married in eight weeks! Few, however, would have been in a position to save up enough to buy the all-important engagement ring. Once the pair had established that marriage was what they both wanted, the young man sought out an opportunity to ask the girl's parents or guardian for their permission. One rarely heard of the request being refused; if it was, then it was likely that, provided the girl was over the age of consent, the couple would go ahead anyway. That would probably have involved a family rift, the girl leaving home and missing out on all the preparations involved in the period up to the wedding.

The Miss who had followed the conventional path was now proudly displaying her lovely new engagement ring. Well, it might be new to her but bearing in mind the cost involved in the purchase, some girls were quite happy to accept a second-hand one. It might have come from a shop – pawnbrokers often had unredeemed ones for sale – but often the future bridegroom offered his loved one a ring that had been in his family; perhaps it had once belonged to his grandmother or his mother, a tradition carried on in more recent times in the royal family. Quite often the couple chose the ring together and were frequently seen on a Saturday afternoon, hand-in-hand, gazing into the windows of H. Samuel's, the affordable jewellers, where it was possible in 1950 to buy a three-diamond ring from their second-hand range for £25. Bravingtons, another well-known jewellers, presented the couple who purchased a wedding ring – and it was usually just the one for the bride, the idea of an exchange of rings came later – with a free gift. How many 1950s brides still have at least one of the six silver-plated teaspoons that Bravingtons gave them?

She has probably dropped enough hints that what she wants is marriage.

The now extinct Woolworths was an option for those with little money for, in the days before stores were arranged on an open plan, among the many deep maroon-painted counters there was one devoted to jewellery. There it was possible to choose from a wide selection of rings, which included the all-important wedding band. Many a young girl would have tried on a Woolies ring in order to decide which style would best suit her hand when the time came. And when it did, if she did settle for a 'fashion' ring, she was promised that it would be replaced with the real thing when the couple's economic situation improved. With luck that would be before the 'gold' had tarnished. As in everything else, fashion dictated the current designs for rings, with new shapes chosen for the setting of the jewel. The solitaire diamond remained a favourite for many, but others opted for rubies, sapphires and emeralds, all of which had imitation versions, while the more daring went for unusual stones, perhaps one associated with a birthstone. Brave indeed was the girl who chose either an opal or a pearl. If she had a superstitious mother she would be warned that the gift of an opal indicated a changeable nature, while the pearl was said to bring tears. A sharp intake of breath from mother and the marriage was doomed before it started!

2

Something New, Something Borrowed ...

During the period between the engagement and the wedding, saving became the watchword for most couples. This often meant that they severely curtailed their social life, twice-weekly visits to the cinema were cut to one and even that might have to alternate with the Saturday night dance. With both of them still living at home, they were expected to follow the family's house rules, going home after work for their evening meal before meeting up. Most parents expected their sons and daughters, engaged or not, to be home by half past ten at the latest during the week. In those days most cinema performances ended just after ten o'clock and if one was dependent on public transport the last trolley bus or tram was likely to be not many minutes after that. The closeness of the end of a film and the last bus meant leaving the cinema as quickly possible to secure a place in the bus queue, but to do that you had to get out before having to stand for the National Anthem. The whole of the first verse was played and people who dared to walk out before it had finished were severely frowned upon. If you missed the bus, then it meant a long walk home and possibly an irate parent waiting when you got there. Girls rarely had a key to let themselves in but the parents of young men were somewhat more tolerant in allowing that after their son had taken his fiancée home, he was bound to be home closer to eleven o'clock. A concession was made if it was known that the couple was going to a Saturday dance which, by law, had to finish at midnight. If the pair then dawdled home because there was no transport, it might be nearly two o'clock by the time the chap reached his own home. One astute young man soon realised that if he timed his arrival home just before the Westminster chiming clock in the living room struck once for the quarter, he could be sure that, if he had disturbed his mother's sleep, when she asked over breakfast, 'and what time did you get in last night?' he would be able to answer in all honesty that it had struck one just after he came in.

Occasionally, instead of going out, the couple would stay in during the evening, most often at the girl's home where they might be offered the chance to sit in 'the front room', 'parlour' or whatever the room was called that contained the three-piece suite, the potted plant, china cabinet, a folding card table with a green baize top, a selection of dull paintings and grim photographs and possibly the piano. This room was usually used only on Sundays, when you had visitors or at Christmas time, and in those days before central heating

Worse was the giggly little sister listening for times when the conversation stopped, a sure sign the couple was kissing.

became the norm it was rarely heated except for special occasions. A single bar of the electric fire might be turned on if it was chilly, but parents were likely to remind you about the cost of electricity. In the depth of winter when snow was on the ground, mother might take a shovelful of burning coals from the fire in the living room and, carefully holding the end of the shovel against a metal dustpan for safety, transfer it to the grate in the front room where it was banked up with one more shovelful of coal. When that had died down almost to ash, it was time for the young man to go home.

The problem with staying in was that one could be plagued by younger members of the family, such as the 12-year-old sister who suddenly remembered she hadn't done her piano practice, or the 11-year-old brother who barged in to ask for male help with the algebraic equations with which he was wrestling. Worse was the giggly little sister who stood in the hall listening for times when the conversation stopped, a sure sign the couple was kissing. That particular child had been told to learn the Ten Commandments by heart for Sunday School, so when she heard silence, she opened the door and confronting the pair, who had quickly jumped apart in embarrassment, intoned in a sombre voice, 'Thou shalt not commit adultery!' So often in the 1950s, children did not receive satisfactory information on certain subjects. The child had been told, when she asked her Sunday School teacher the meaning of 'adultery', that it was 'something grown-ups did'. The reader can imagine the hullabaloo that broke out after, the bride-to-be screaming to her mother to remove the offending child, who was promptly given a 'good talking to' and sent straight to bed. In retrospect, it's possible that the bride-to-be was not totally certain of the meaning either.

While the pair were busy saving what they could from their weekly wages, the girl started collecting for her 'bottom drawer'. This was a hangover from the distant past when part of a bride's dowry took the form of her coming to the marriage with bed and table linen, cutlery and china sufficient to equip the new home. By Victorian times this had been expanded to what became known as a 'trousseau' and included the bride's wedding dress and other clothes. In some cases all these items were carefully stored in the wooden box familiarly known as a hope chest. Amongst the upper classes it had become a tradition, up until the Second World War, that every bride would have a full set of matching table and bed linen as well as several sets of nightgowns and underwear. It was customary for these tò be embroidered, the linen with the initials of the bride and groom, the undergarments with pretty motifs. The sewing was usually done by a member of the household staff, the lady's maid or the ageing nanny who no longer had any children to look after but was hoping she would come into her own again once young Miss started her own family. Amongst those middle-class girls who were not employed outside the home, embroidering lingerie and nightdresses was a pleasant pastime. The more ambitious girl might actually make items such as blouses.

The average working girl in the 1950s could not expect her parents to lay up a store of bed linen, even if they could afford it, for at the beginning of the decade such items were still in short supply, having only been taken off rationing in 1947. Many girls learned how to 'make do and mend' as they watched or helped their mothers put 'sides to middle'. Since cotton sheets receive most of their wear in the middle, after years of use plus the constant boiling, either at home or by a laundry, the centre portion became very thin, in danger of becoming so threadbare it would disintegrate into holes. Once a sheet was beyond the stage where it could be patched or darned, both of which could prove to feel scratchy to the skin, then more drastic measures were required. The sheet was cut in half longways and the two outer edges were machined together with a 'run and fell' seam which guaranteed that it would hold together firmly. Unfortunately, the good economic housewife did not always take into account the fact that trying to sleep on this seam was very uncomfortable, especially if the sheets were made of heavy cotton. Once turned, the new edges were trimmed and then carefully hemmed to prevent fraying.

But what did our 1950s bride put in her 'bottom drawer' which wasn't always literally at the bottom of the chest of drawers in her bedroom? A Saturday afternoon shopping trip in town with her best girlfriend gave her the chance to look for the more mundane items which would be necessary in her new home. Woolworths was the ideal place to search for reasonably priced objects like the latest in tin openers, tea strainers, egg cups, whisks and other kitchen necessities like a rolling pin and pastry cutters, a frying pan and milk saucepan, a cheese grater and perhaps, if she had saved enough that week, a whole set of matching kitchen implements with their blue-, yellow- or red-painted handles that had a hole near the end by which to hang the implement up. These last were really modern – while her mother would have always mashed potatoes with a dinner fork, our 1950s bride could buy a masher plus a couple of other items for which she had yet to discover a use. Woolworths also did a very nice line in china and glassware, so she bought things that took her fancy, knowing that she would be able to go back later to complete the set. Many a girl filled the omissions in her wedding presents with Woolies ware. The larger department stores, old established family businesses whose names they bore, also provided a happy hunting ground for our future bride. It was here that the bride may have looked at the limited range of bridal wear on offer, deciding what style of dress she would wear for her big day. She might also go into one of the smaller shops that sold ladies' clothing. Here there were specific areas devoted to coats, dresses and formal wear, which included a very small selection of evening gowns, lingerie, hats and gloves. The problem with these shops was that you couldn't just browse and then blatantly walk out, you were expected at least to try something on – and make a purchase – and it was very difficult to avoid the firm but civil assistant who wanted to know the moment you walked in what exactly it was Madam was looking for.

Those who married in the first few years of the 1950s had far less choice than those who followed in the second half of the decade. This applied not only to the dress but also to the way the marriage was celebrated. Nowadays it seems that the first booking made is for the venue of the reception. Once that is fixed, then, if the actual ceremony is to be in church, the local vicar is approached in the hope that he and the church are free on the chosen day. Then follow all the other arrangements: booking the cars, the photographers, arranging for the video recording, printing invitations and service sheets, bouquets for the bridal party, flowers for church and venue, not to mention choosing the menus for the wedding breakfast and the buffet refreshments for the evening party, booking the disco for the latter and, of course, deciding on the all-important cake – or cakes. No wonder it is said to cost a fortune to get married these days and take at least two years in the planning.

Back in the 1950s most people married in church. This didn't necessarily mean the couple were both regular churchgoers, though their parents often were, but apart from the Registrar's Office, the only people licensed to perform marriages were priests of the Church of England, and unless one received special dispensation the marriage could only take place in the parish church of one of the couple, most usually the bride. This legal requirement harked right back through history to the days when newly married couples appeared at the church door to be seen by passers-by who might later be asked to testify that the marriage had actually taken place. An early eighteenth-century Marriage Act upheld the necessity for local residency of three weeks before the wedding could take place in an effort to crack down on quickie marriages by unlicensed priests. Only a special licence could bypass the twenty-one-day rule. In church this took the form of the reading of the banns of marriage for the three Sundays before the wedding. The couple were expected to attend to listen as the vicar read out their full names. Often this was the first time that the couple were made aware of the other's second or third names. This could come as a shock, especially if you had always known your intended as Mitch, Hank or Jack, to discover that he was really Cuthbert or Arbuthnot, and equally for him to find he was not marrying Angela but Agnes. As Agnes/Angela listened to the words 'spinster of this parish' she would sigh with relief, comforting herself that very soon that dreaded word would never again be applied to her. On the other hand, there was just a tinge of fear that someone might jump up and declare there was 'an impediment' as to why she should not be married. Has anyone, I wonder, ever attended a wedding where, when those words were repeated, an objection was made? Nowadays it seems to happen only in soap operas.

Of course it was quite possible for a couple who were Nonconformists or of another religious faith to marry in their particular place of worship, provided that the Registrar's Office was properly informed beforehand. In these cases, a Registrar came to the ceremony, supervised the signing of the register and issued the official marriage certificate. Those wishing to have a simpler, civil ceremony often opted to go to the Registry Office itself. These included those couples in which one party was divorced, since they could not be married in a church anyway. Sometimes too, if the bride-to-be had been widowed, it was felt to be more appropriate for her second wedding to be a quiet one – and of course she certainly could not appear in a white wedding gown!

So, back to that all-important dress. Bearing in mind that austerity still lingered, many brides took the option of borrowing a dress. This might even be her mother's, although the 1920s wedding dress did not suit the fashion of the time – oddly enough by the end of the 1950s the length would have been right, if not much else. So better to forget mum's dress and borrow from a recently married friend or relation and placate mum by asking if you could borrow her veil and headdress instead. The second option was to have a dress made. If mother was good with her needle and sewing machine then she would make it. Few homes from the 1930s and '40s were complete without a Singer sewing machine whether it be grandma's treadle one or the hand-driven portable one. The one required co-ordination between the feet, which were pedalling, and the hands, both of which were steering the material, while the second left only one hand free to feed the material while the other turned the handle. The more sophisticated electric sewing machine has solved both these problems but they were yet to come. In the meantime, mother or even the bride herself might make not only *the* dress but those for the bridesmaids and outfits for the pageboys too. There were several advantages to this apart from the cost, it being much cheaper to make than buy; mother and daughter could pore over patterns and material samples together and the final result would be unique, even if a Simplicity or Butterick pattern had inspired it. The dresses would also fit their wearers perfectly, and colours and materials would all match. If she was no home dressmaker, then the bride had the option of having the dress (or dresses) made by a professional. Every town, and village too, had ladies, often widowed with a family to support, who had set up businesses in their own home. These clever seamstresses were able to look at pictures in a magazine or pattern book and put the neckline of one on to the bodice of another and join that to the skirt of a third. The bride would buy the material of her choice

Has anyone, I wonder, ever attended a wedding where, when those words were repeated, an objection was made?

and her gown would be made up for her at a fraction of the cost of a bought one. When it came to buying dresses, unless the bride and her family could afford it, it was tactfully suggested that the bridesmaids should pay for their own. If this was the case, then the bride needed to be even more tactful in suggesting what she would like them to wear. If the bridesmaid was thinking her dress could double as an evening dress later, then she was unlikely to want an unusual colour or material. Most brides played safe by opting to have their attendants in pink, blue or yellow – rarely green as that was considered an unlucky colour. But, as we all know, there are many shades within a colour and so, for example, the bridesmaid cousins who lived miles apart might well turn up for duty in anything from aquamarine and turquoise to dusty pink or deep rose. Taffeta and crêpe were the materials that were much in vogue in the first half of the decade.

In the latter years of the 1950s, with the growth in manufacturing and the introduction of new materials, alongside an easing of the economic situation and the influence of America through the cinema, fashion was changing. Fewer brides chose the traditional full-length figured brocade gown with a small train, opting instead for the ballerina-style dress à la Audrey Hepburn. One bride who married in Cumberland (Cumbria) in January 1956 had such a dress. Made by her aunt for a total of £18, it had the three-quarter-length skirt with the nipped-in waist, long sleeves, and was trimmed with swansdown. For summer brides, both floral organdie and broderie anglaise were popular, as were layers of tulle over stiffened net petticoats. There was a much more modern feel now to weddings. Gone were the very large bouquets such as Princess Elizabeth had for her wedding. More often than not these had been the virginal white lily or dramatic red carnations or roses with lots of trailing maidenhair fern, while in autumn bronze chrysanthemums were a popular choice, as they also were for funeral wreaths. These were now supplanted by neat posies of more delicate flowers such as tiny pink rosebuds with lily of the valley. Our Cumbrian bride carried a prayer book to which was attached by a silk ribbon a small spray of roses and freesias. A tip for relations looking over old family albums, when faced with random wedding photographs it is often as easy to give a rough estimate of their dates by the style and type of flowers that were carried as by the dresses worn.

Entertaining the guests was always an important consideration. First there was the vital question of who should be invited. Throughout the 1950s it seems to have been taken for granted that most of the relations would be invited even if Auntie Violet hadn't spoken to Uncle Bill since that trouble over Great-Aunt Maud's will. Should you include all the cousins; would one lot be disappointed if they were left out? And was it right that the bridegroom's family wanted more guests than the bride's? This was likely to bring about strong mutterings from the bride's father on the subject of who was paying for this anyway. As the lists grew, there was only one way out of the dilemma and that was to hold the wedding on a weekday when most people would be at work and therefore unable to attend! However, few were unlikely to take such drastic action, and they would certainly not choose a Friday, which, as everyone knew, was an unlucky day to get married – almost as inauspicious as the bride who 'changed her name but not the letter'.

The venue for the wedding breakfast, as it was still known in some areas – another historical hangover – in the early 1950s, was most likely to be in a local hall. In those far-off days when hardly anyone had a car, it was essential that the hall should be as close as possible to the church so that guests could comfortably stroll to it after the service. It really wouldn't do to have one's friends and relations all dressed up in their Sunday best having to travel any distance on the local bus, so a hall attached to the church or chapel or village hall was ideal. Also popular was the 'function' room upstairs in a convenient public house. All these tended to be very basic in their design: walls whitewashed or painted dark green or brown, floors dusty wooden boards or covered with pre-war patterned lino, faded with time and wear. On the walls of each of these hung pictures suitable to their normal usage: religious ones for the Sunday School, Mothers' Union or Sisterhood; illustrative material for the Scouts, Guides, Cubs and Brownies; and always, it seemed, sombre, sepia portraits of ministers, rectors, founding fathers of organisations from Victorian times, all of them bewhiskered and forbidding. The room over the pub was probably worse; the portraits here were similar although their gentlemen subjects all appeared, to the casual observer to be in fancy dress, and somewhere close to them would be displayed a pair of gigantic buffalo horns. The biggest drawback aesthetically speaking was the overriding smell of beer and the thick coating of nicotine on the ceiling. But somehow, none of this was a real drawback. A vase or two of flowers, perhaps some coloured crêpe paper streamers across the ceiling, would soon brighten the place up.

Much more important was what food was going to be served. It has to be remembered that rationing of some foods was in operation until as late as 1954. Although tinned and dried fruit, chocolate biscuits, black treacle and golden syrup as well as jellies and mincemeat were de-rationed in 1950, this did not mean that they were all immediately available. Thus, although a 1950s bride would have the dried fruit needed to make the wedding cake and flour, which had been off ration for two years, the other basic ingredients of butter (including margarine), sugar and eggs were still subject to rationing until 1953. Tea had been decontrolled the previous year but meat, bacon and cheese had to wait until 1954. The one saving grace for those catering for a wedding was that they were allowed up to 2lb of ham – so no prizes for guessing what featured on many a wedding menu.

Although this book is intended to be about the women who became wives during the 1950s, we must not forget the tremendous role played by those women who were already wives; that is, their mothers. These were women who had been tested to the full: bringing up families – most of them single-handed if their husbands were in the armed forces – often in the most trying circumstances, coping with all the pressures put on them by the Second World War and the immediate years that followed. Many of them had had their own childhood affected by the First World War and their early married life by the Depression, so perhaps in some way they were prepared for whatever else life threw at them. Children of the 1930s and '40s probably only appreciated just how much their mothers did in keeping the home going, feeding and clothing them on very little, when they themselves were faced with making economies. Let us all say a silent thank you to all the mothers who scrimped and saved, and particularly those who organised their daughters' weddings. These mothers relied on a close network of friends and relations for help with the provision and preparation of the food. Donations of essential ingredients for the baking; precious tins of peaches that had been carefully hoarded for an emergency; fresh cream and eggs; even a chicken or two from farming relations to eke out the ubiquitous ham; fresh vegetables and the essential lettuces and tomatoes from friendly allotment holders – all gifts were most gratefully received. This type of 1950s wedding reception certainly lacked uniformity. There was little concern about co-ordination, colour or otherwise, whether it be for the china and cutlery, which was borrowed, or portion control. The different ladies who made the trifles supplied the dish in which it was served and followed their own particular methods. Hence some could be heavily weighted with sponge cake and little fruit, while others had a thick layer of jelly under the custard and they didn't all have a fresh cream topping. It was customary for the bride's mother, once the food had all been assembled and the tables laid, to secure the best-looking trifle for the bridal party at the top table.

Most weddings took place in the early afternoon, so that gave mother and her helpers the morning to prepare the feast. Trestle tables were set out as three sides of a square and covered with a number of borrowed white tablecloths with the occasional sheet to make up any deficiency. A vase or two of flowers down the centre of the table and then mismatched cutlery, a plate and a wine glass marked each place, complemented by a carefully handwritten (or typed if the bride worked in an office) card bearing a guest's name. Just as today, hours had been spent deciding who should sit next to whom. In those early days, the meal tended to consist of a main course – meat and vegetables or salad – followed by a dessert (or afters) such as the aforementioned trifle, tinned fruit, apple pie and custard. If it was a winter wedding, then soup might be served and a hot baked potato added to the plate of cold meats. There would have been wine – Sauterne was very popular – and orange squash for the young and abstainers. Speeches and toasts were made, then came the cutting of the cake, one or two tiers of a rich fruit mixture covered in white icing with a simple piped decoration. Small slices of cake were then served along with cups of tea – coffee drinking was still very much in its infancy in the provinces before the mid-1950s.

Let us all say a silent thank you to all the mothers who scrimped and saved, and particularly those who organised their daughters' weddings.

Once the meal was over, tables were cleared and chairs moved back to walls to allow guests to move around and talk or perhaps look at the gifts the bride and groom had received. In those days, the ordinary couple did not send out a list with the wedding invitation describing the items they hoped to receive, neither did they have an arrangement with large department stores to hold their list. The only indication of preferences came when the couple had decided they liked a certain design in china or cutlery and they would discreetly inform whoever asked that they would like such and such design of tea or dinner service, available at Bloggs & Sons. This left the giver free to decide what he or she could afford, six cups and saucers or maybe only the milk jug and slop basin. For those readers unfamiliar with the latter, if your grandmother still has a china tea service tucked away, it's the bowl you might have mistaken as being for sugar. But no, in those dim and distant days, tea was made by placing loose leaves in a warmed teapot, on to which was poured freshly boiled water. After being left 'to draw' for some minutes, it was poured into the cup through a strainer, usually chrome but it could be silver. When the cup was returned for a second pouring, the dregs of the first cup were drained into the slop basin and a fresh cup poured. Tea strainers rarely surfaced as wedding presents but teapots often did. One lucky bride received not one but eighteen assorted pots. She kept her family supplied with replacements for years. The modern list does do away with duplication. It was a perennial joke that most couples ended up with at least three toast racks or, later on, a couple of electric toasters. What most couples needed were the basic essentials: sheets, pillowcases, blankets, an eiderdown (if one was lucky enough to have a wealthy relation), towels and tablecloths, cutlery and a clock, saucepans and dishes, particularly Pyrex as the decade wore on. However, they were actually likely to end up with several sets of silver-plated fish eaters, delicate plated dessert spoons, cake forks and coffee spoons embellished with a coloured representation of a coffee bean at the end of their fragile handles, all still in their original imitation leather boxes. All these dated from the 1930s or earlier when they had been received as wedding presents by now elderly relations. Unused and unwanted they were handed on. We call it recycling. Much of it is now valuable, so the 1950s bride may regret that, finding it not to her taste, she passed it on to another couple when a shortage of money meant she could ill afford to buy them a gift.

Sometimes, when the hall was close enough to the bride's home, guests would be invited there to see the display of gifts, all neatly arranged with the donors' cards bearing their names beside each one. Having viewed and discussed the presents, for some the wedding reception was now over. Only close family and friends were likely to stay on, for many had buses or trains to catch to distant destinations or young children to collect from whoever had looked after them for the afternoon. The bride and groom too disappeared, and while the remaining guests chatted, perhaps over another drink, the newlyweds went home to change into their going-away outfits, ready to set off for their honeymoon. The new husband might actually keep on the suit he had been wearing but if he was a serviceman and had married in his uniform – that always looked good in the photographs – then he would change into a suit. The bride's outfit was always chosen with great care for it was expected to last her for a year or two, so if it was winter, she would choose a stylish winter coat and a pretty dress or skirt and blouse, with matching shoes and handbag as well as, of course, gloves and a hat. Another good standby was what was known then as a costume but now as a suit; a good tailored affair, preferably in the latest fashion, as it had to last. This too would be completed by, as the local newspaper report of the wedding would have it, 'the matching accessories'.

The bridal pair would then re-emerge in the hall to say their farewells. Someone would have found a car to drive them to the station to catch their train. Suitably beribboned at the front and with an old boot and a couple of tin cans trailing from the back, the car carried them off amongst the cheers of well-wishers, but not before the bride had thrown her bouquet behind her towards the anxiously waiting young females who hoped they might be next. In my home town the station platform for the 6.30 p.m. train to London was usually crowded on a Saturday, not with passengers but with those very close friends who, having made sure they had purchased the requisite platform ticket from the machine for 1*d*, had come to wave off all the newlyweds, showering them first with confetti as they set off to spend their first night together as a married couple. Over the years the Great Eastern Hotel at Liverpool Street must have witnessed many hundreds of young people setting off not only to their honeymoon destinations but also on the greatest adventure of their lives.

Obviously, much of the foregoing is full of generalities as no two weddings were ever exactly the same. Much depended on the financial circumstances of the family. Since it was customary for the father of the bride to pay for the reception as well as other expenses – and there were little books of rather outdated etiquette which explained who paid for what – if he had sufficient savings for this day, the whole thing would have been different. Moving slightly up the social scale would have been the sit-down meal of three courses in a local restaurant or hotel, with the cake ordered from a professional baker. In 1956 it was possible to have such a reception for thirty guests for £50. It would have been a bit more formal than the one described earlier, but again, all over within the afternoon. An alternative to this was the sort of affair which involved standing around with nothing more than a glass or two of champagne and a selection of canapés – a terrible disappointment for guests who had travelled halfway across the country by train, had eaten nothing since breakfast, and could not afford the dining car on the return journey. Never would a bag of chips have tasted so good, even if the chip shop owner would have been somewhat taken aback by the arrival of floral-hatted and white-gloved customers. Those who had the space and money were able to hold the reception in a marquee in their garden. Responsibility for the smooth running devolved upon the outside caterers who not only saw to the delivery of the gold- or white-painted chairs and circular tables to hold eight or ten guests each, but also dealt with all the food, providing the staff to serve the meal and wine. Florists would also have been in attendance either the day before or on the morning of the wedding. The whole operation would have been carried out with almost military-style precision, with a master of ceremonies directing who should make the speeches and when. Throughout the meal music would have been provided, perhaps by a string quartet or a solo harpist.

One unfortunate bride was denied any formal pictures of her big day as the groom absolutely refused to stand around being stared at!

To be honest, not many of my contributors experienced this upper end of the market, but from 1956 onwards, it became much more the norm for mother to be relieved of the tremendous responsibility of organising everything. Instead she had the chance to appear cool, calm and lovely in her mother-of-the-bride outfit, which hopefully would not clash with that of the groom's mother, or, even worse, be identical to it. Since most formal wedding photography was in black and white, it didn't really matter for the photographs if the colours they wore screamed at each other. Long before videos, disposable cameras and telephones capable of taking photographs were even dreamed of, the specialist wedding photographer was called upon to take pictures. To guard against misfortunes such as heavy rain, high winds or deep snow, the wedding party would go to the photographer's studio on leaving the church, and there a simple series of formal portraits such as the bride and groom alone – to be reproduced in cabinet size for both sets of parents to frame and hang on the sitting room wall or stand on top of the piano – the bride, groom, their parents, the best man and the bridesmaids, in a smaller size and given to those involved and close relations, would be taken. If money was no object then an album was also purchased. The professional might also attend at the church to take going-in and coming-out pictures, but on no account would he be allowed to disturb the service with his camera. One unfortunate bride was denied any formal pictures of her big day as the groom absolutely refused to stand around being stared at! As the decade progressed and film became readily available, pre-war box Brownie cameras came into their own for a while, only to be supplanted by smaller, more up-to-date models, and soon guests were happily snapping away while the professional did his job. Fortunately, none of this took as much time as the modern photographic session appears to do and it wasn't long before the guests could go off to shake hands with the bridal party, drink a glass of red or white wine before sitting down to a prawn cocktail, chicken Kiev or roast beef with vegetables in season followed by peach melba or the ever-popular sherry trifle, and then by cheese and biscuits and coffee.

There were those receptions, usually held in late afternoon, where, following the meal, cake cutting and so forth, there would be a period when the guests would leave the tables and mingle while the newlyweds would circulate throughout the room talking to as many of the guests as possible. For some this was the time to slip away, for others it was a chance to light up their cigarettes or for some men a chance to visit the bar for a beer. The women tended to make for the 'Ladies', to repair their make-up and discuss their true opinion about the whole proceedings so far. Once the tables had been cleared it was time for the dancing to begin, with the bride and groom circling the floor several times on their own – an embarrassing time for some. Music might be provided by a small three-piece band or simply a friend with a record player and a collection of 78 and 45 records. The days of the deafening disco and the separate evening party for all one's young friends that caused ageing relations to wish that they had left earlier had yet to come. As had the sophisticated 'stag' weekend; most young men would have met up for a few drinks with their closest friends a night or two before their wedding but it would have been a casual arrangement. As for the term 'hen party', that was totally unknown in the 1950s.

Like so many things during the decade, the honeymoon was shaped by whether it took place before or after 1956. Those who honeymooned after that date had options that would have seemed unbelievable in 1950. They could, if they wished, go abroad, not just by ferry boat to France and then on by train to places in Europe like Austria, but on two-week package holidays by air offered by newly set up holiday companies. This was indeed an exciting prospect. With hindsight it now seems laughable. Passengers booked in at Victoria in London and were then conveyed with their luggage to, for example, Blackbushe Airport, a converted RAF base on the Surrey–Hampshire border. There was still a feeling of austerity about the single-storey building, through which the travellers passed straight on to the landing strip. On their way to the waiting aircraft they would have gone past one of those huge red weighing machines with a dial, manned by a uniformed member of staff who scrutinised everyone and, presumably working on an average weight ratio, would publicly weigh anyone who looked overweight! The planes themselves were small and slow in comparison with those of today, and rather scary, so there was a good excuse to clasp your partner's hand tightly as you sucked on your barley sugar sweet during take-off.

At popular times of the year, these holiday flights could be filled almost entirely with the recently married, especially those who had married before 5 April, as this allowed a bridegroom to claim the married man's allowance for the whole of the previous tax year, bringing him a substantial tax rebate. On the subject of money, in 1957 a fortnight's package holiday by air to the Italian Riviera cost about £30 per person. This took some saving and, of course, there was also the need to have some spending money for incidentals like drinks and ice creams. Fortunately, the amount you had available to spend while you were away was limited not just by your own personal financial situation, but by no lesser person than the Chancellor of the Exchequer. Travellers abroad were not allowed to take more than £30 sterling out of the country. When purchasing traveller's cheques or foreign currency, a note of the amount was made in your passport; once that had gone there was no going to the bank or using a credit card (they were not in everyday use anyway) to draw more, so one had to learn to be economical.

Package holidays apart, the latter years of the 1950s also brought to the fore the use of cars. Car ownership was still very limited but petrol was now freely available, so it was often possible for a young couple either to hire or be loaned the use of a car. For these lucky ones, they still tended to follow the trend of making for the seaside for their honeymoon, though occasionally the local press, when giving a detailed report of a wedding, would add those magical, mysterious words, 'the honeymoon is to be spent touring', which certainly didn't imply an organised trip by coach, but rather a two-seater sports car and Scotland or the Lake District. One couple described driving to Italy to stay in the villa of an uncle, while another honeymooned in that most romantic of cities, Paris. Those who had married between 1950 and 1955 tended to have only a week away. The most likely destination was the seaside, and since money was a major concern this was often in a resort not that far away from home. A great advantage of living in the British Isles is that the coast is so accessible. Those brides who did not wish to be disappointed in their holiday destination either made suggestions as to where they wanted to go or dropped very broad hints if the husband-to-be was making the arrangements – unlike the bride who was promised a great surprise, only to find herself whisked off to a nearby resort that she particularly disliked. That certainly did not make for the easiest of starts to married life.

Accommodation for the week at the seaside was most likely to be in a bed and breakfast, hotel or boarding house. These acquired a reputation of being run by fearsome landladies who ruled the place with the proverbial rod. They were not the best of places for a young couple to stay as, having eaten breakfast, they were expected to vacate the premises and not return until the evening. And should they wish to return after 10.30 p.m. following a visit to the theatre or cinema, they had to inform the landlady and ask for a key. Although there would have been a washbasin in the bedroom, there was, of course, no such thing as an en suite bathroom; the one down the hall was shared with the other guests. There was no such thing either as a shower, and in some places you had to pay extra to have a bath, possibly having to place a 1s coin in the meter that provided the gas for the geyser that heated the water. All in all the accommodation could be pretty cheerless. But you were young and in love and provided the weather was reasonable, you really didn't mind.

If funds stretched that far then a hotel offered slightly more luxury – though you still didn't have your own bathroom! An alternative that provided accommodation and full board as well as lots of entertainment throughout the day was Butlins or one of the smaller holiday camps dotted around the country, and many couples chose these. But a cheaper option to all these was to go to stay with relations, preferably fairly young ones that you liked, either in the country or, if you hankered for the bright lights, theatres, and museums and art galleries, then what could be better than the aunts or cousins who lived close to London. Hop on a bus or take the Tube, an experience in itself for those from the provinces, and there was a whole world waiting to be discovered.

Aftre all discovery was what a honeymoon was all about in those far-off days. This was the first opportunity the majority had to find out much about the other that had been hidden – not least what lay beneath their clothing. It is not a cliché to say that most girls had never seen a man naked. Suddenly two people are put together sharing a bedroom and having to decide who sleeps on which side of the bed. This was the time when illusions could be shattered: that beautiful curly hair was achieved with the use of metal curlers, his toenails needed cutting and his feet could smell. But for that one week, it didn't really matter, there was a whole lifetime ahead of them to sort out or get used to such things. Come the end of the week, they would be making a home together.

Two Personal Stories

Listening to ladies talking about their early lives and then reading through the answers of others to my questions, it became apparent that despite the contributors being dispersed throughout the country there was a strong similarity in the way they lived, as if there was a pattern that had to be adhered to. There was, however, one contribution that was so very different I felt it merited a special mention. Then came another very detailed account of a courtship and marriage that fitted the more typical picture and somehow the two seemed to belong together.

Jean's Story

Jean was born in Crouch End, London, SH2 in 1930, not the most auspicious of years. The Depression was almost at its height; throughout the country men marched in what became known as Marches for Work as unemployment figures grew from 2 million in August to 2.5 million by December. Life was insecure too for Jean's father but fortunately he had wisely invested his First World War gratuity by buying a large old house. This provided his mother with a flat as well as a home for him and his wife and child, and gave the family an appearance of affluence they did not necessarily have. However, by the time Jean was 5, her father's earnings were sufficient to send his daughter not to the local council school, which would have meant crossing a busy main road, but to the nearby fee-paying convent school. At the outbreak of the Second World War most of London's schoolchildren were evacuated to safer parts of the country and 9-year-old Jean and her younger sister, aged 4, were sent to a convent boarding school in Chard, Somerset. Later, following her studies for the School Certificate Jean returned home to live with her mother in London.

After years in the countryside it was a shock to return, not only to life in the capital but to the harsh reality of having to attend a Junior Labour Exchange to find a job. Helped by this, she found herself working in a large building near Liverpool Street Station where, since the windows were still boarded up following the bombing, she had to work all day in electric light. She hated it, but relief came when the 18-year-old Jean found employment in the offices of the Electricity Board near her home. There she not only found the work more to her taste but within a few months her future would be decided when 22-year-old Jim joined the office staff, newly demobbed from the army. Love blossomed slowly. The office arranged a draw for tickets for a special concert in Haringey Arena featuring the world-famous opera singer Lily Pons and her husband, the conductor and arranger André Kostelanetz, who was well known to music lovers through his many recordings and to the wider British audience generally for his arrangement of *With a Song in my Heart*, the theme tune of the radio programme, *Forces Favourites*. Jean was persuaded to put her name down and was lucky to secure a ticket. The day of the concert Jim announced that quite by chance his seat was next to hers. Those two ticket stubs, dating from 1948, are among Jean's treasures, found following Jim's death just eighteen months short of their diamond wedding anniversary.

They went out together for two years and got engaged on Jean's 20th birthday in 1950. The two-and-a-half-year engagement that followed was the result of their waiting to find somewhere of their own to live. Jean's widowed mother had offered them the top-floor flat in the family home but Jean preferred to wait until they could be truly independent. By this time Jean was working in one of the Electricity Showrooms that used to occupy every main street of towns throughout the country. You would go there to pay your electricity bill, buy a new kettle or a new cooker and, if you were moving house, you would call in to make arrangements to have the supply cut off and the meter read. When Jean mentioned to her mother that she had met a lady she knew making arrangements prior to removal, her mother announced that she would have a word with the landlord of the flat concerned. This was a one-bedroom flat above a builder's premises. Hopes were later dashed when the builder related that he intended to change the flat into offices. It is not often that fate influences bureaucracy, but that was the case when the local planning department turned down the application for change of use and so, several weeks later, the builder handed Jean the keys to what was to become her marital home.

During their engagement the couple had been scouring the shops during the sales in search of bargains. Jim meticulously filed many of the bills from this period so we know, for instance, that in October 1951 they bought a complete bedroom suite for £57 7s 6d plus purchase tax of 10 per cent, making a total of £63 2s 3d. In

April 1952 they bought an Ercol dining room suite with four chairs, two of which were carvers, for £34 6s 8d. In between came orders for curtains and then, a week before the wedding, they bought a three-piece suite in uncut moquette for £57 15s. The illustrations of the receipts show another small detail of 1950s life that has long gone and been mostly forgotten too, that of the seller of the goods signing over a twopenny stamp to show that the bill had been paid.

By the time of the actual wedding on 14 June 1952 the flat was almost furnished and ready to move into. Their wedding presents also provided many useful items. Again Jim made a note of them, including the pressure cooker from his brother and a carpet sweeper from a friend of Jean's mother's. I mentioned to Jean that although some of her colleagues attended the wedding, I was surprised that they had not come up with a joint gift of a vacuum cleaner as one might have expected from the Electricity Showroom staff. She explained that they certainly would not have been able to afford it and in any case that just wasn't done in those days. She went on to state that she had bought their first cleaner, an Electrolux 55 cylinder model – and that had lasted over twenty years!

A reception for about forty people was held at Jean's home, not in a marquee in the garden as Diana had in the following year. The two-tier wedding cake was bought from a local baker and proved to be almost inedible, and the standard buffet of the time was provided by outside caterers. After the reception the couple left for a week in Sidmouth in Devon, the bride wearing a pale green linen two-piece, complete with hat, handbag and gloves. The following week they were at last in their very own home and it was back to work for them both. Jean had become a 1950s housewife.

Diana's Story

Jean and Diana have much in common: they were both born in London, from which they were evacuated during the war, and both went to boarding school. They are of similar age, give or take a year or so, and they married within a year of each other, Jean in 1952 and Diana in 1953. But while Jean's story mirrors many of their generation, Diana's certainly does not. It could, in so many ways, have come straight from the pages of one of the romantic novels that were serialised in women's magazines of the period. To begin with Diana's background was very different to that of the average girl of the period. Her father was a solicitor with a practice in Fenchurch Street in London, and her family home was in a fashionable part of Hampstead. Just one of the many pointers as to how out of the ordinary her family was was the fact that her mother could, and did, drive a car. Like Jean, Diana spent some of the war years out of London, eventually going to boarding school in Abbots Bromley. Like Jean she sat for her School Certificate but then she followed the path of other girls of her social background and took a course at the prestigious St James's Secretarial College in London. Her first job was in a travel agent's. In the first half of 1953, when Diana was just 20 years old, her carefree social life, which included membership of the Young Conservatives, of which she became branch treasurer, and the local tennis club, changed dramatically; but let her recall exactly what happened:

It was a very cold evening in early April and the house was pretty chaotic because I was hosting a meeting of the local Y Cs that included a table tennis tournament. At the same time my parents who were holding a bridge party were waiting for two elderly ladies to join them. They duly arrived, having been brought by a chap I'd never met before. Mother invited him to come in and offered him a cold drink, which was the last thing he wanted on a cold night. It turned out after a rather hurried conversation that he was home on leave from Nigeria where he had been working for the past four years. Being so busy with other things, I really didn't give him much attention. I later found out from my parents that they knew his father and stepmother from church, so when he called to ask me out, they were quite agreeable to my spending time with him. I think that Robert, who at twenty-seven was older than most of the young men friends I had, had already decided that it was time he found himself a wife. So over the next two or three weeks he invited me to, among other things, the theatre to see 'South Pacific', to watch the Boat Race and – somehow, he had even managed to get seats in Park Lane for the Coronation!

During those first few weeks Robert proposed two or three times – but it had all happened so quickly, it didn't seem possible. Then I was invited to join Robert and his parents for a week's holiday in Guernsey. One day he and I went by ourselves on a boat trip across to Sark and there, in that most romantic setting, with him producing the ring he had bought earlier in St Peter Port, Robert again asked me to marry him and that time I said yes.

We were engaged for just three weeks! We married on 6 June, three days after the Coronation, almost exactly eight weeks since we'd first met. Somehow I managed to go up to Harrods to buy a wedding dress and I had two bridesmaids and a pageboy to carry my train. I was so lucky. I am afraid I left it all to my parents to make all the arrangements – and pay for it all! We had a marquee in the garden and my parents invited many of their friends to a champagne reception. There was one hilarious moment that actually made the pages of the local newspaper. Amongst the male guests, most of whom wore morning dress, there appeared a tall man with a black beard, who was rather conspicuous in a tweed suit. He was on his second glass of champagne when my mother realised she did not know who he was. Although clearly a gatecrasher, he announced himself as the Earl of Davenport. Happily, he left quietly.

Like everything else, our honeymoon was also short, just three days at Sonning-on-Thames. I wore a black and white check dress for my going-away outfit. Then it was a busy time packing up for Nigeria. Under normal circumstances, Robert would have flown back at the end of his leave, but he arranged with his employers, Unilever, for us both to travel to Africa by an Elder Dempster mail boat. It took about thirteen days, so I suppose you could say we had our honeymoon then.

Unlike my friends who married and stayed in England, I had no say in our first home. We were given a Company house in an expatriot compound in Ibadan. The furniture was pretty basic and came with the house. I did not have to cook either, which was fortunate as I couldn't, because the Company provided a local cook who produced wonderful meals cooked on a wood-burning stove. We also had a gardener and a houseboy who did all the domestic work including the washing in a tub. As it was so hot and humid there was always plenty of laundry for him to do. It was hard at first to adjust to life in West Africa. There were very few shops and very little to do all day apart from coffee mornings with other European wives and playing tennis or golf later in the cool of the early evening, or swimming in the clubhouse pool. So I was a stay-at-home wife until I managed to get a job with Rediffusion the worldwide company responsible for setting up and operating radio networks.

In many ways my life was far more restricted than it would have been in England. For example, women did not drive out there, so even though I could drive and we had a car, I could not use it. Apart from the occasional visit to the open-air cinema, our main social life was entertaining at home. It would be several years later that I found out what it was like to be a proper 1950s housewife and by that time I had become a 1950s mother.

3

A Home of Their Own

xcept that it wasn't! At the end of the war in 1945, Britain was faced with an acute housing shortage in those large towns and cities that had suffered severe bomb damage. Often whole streets had been totally wiped out, while others that had been left were declared unsafe as a result of bomb blast. Attempts were made to repair as many of these as possible but there was still a big gap between the number of houses available and the numbers of those who needed them. The obvious solution was to build more, but that was not as easy as it sounds as building materials, particularly timber, were still in very short supply, so all new building was subject to various sorts of regulations and builders required licences to carry out operations. An illustration of the implications of what this could mean came when the daughter of an old established builder married in 1947. Her father gave her a piece of land and offered to build her the house of her dreams. Unfortunately the Ministry of Works and she did not share the same vision, and so she found that the size of her house was greatly reduced, endeding up with a detached version of a small 1930s suburban semi standing on a very large plot. Quite apart from replacing the original housing stock, the increased demand for homes had been exacerbated by the demobilisation of the armed forces and an upsurge in marriages. Then there were the couples who had married during the war where the wife had either remained at home with her parents or had been in lodgings close to where her husband was serving. They now joined the queue of young couples who were searching for somewhere to call home.

Renting your home had been traditional in this country for endless generations. Only the very wealthy few actually owned property and, certainly since the early nineteenth century, it had been commonplace for both landowners and industrialists to provide their workers with housing for which a weekly rent was paid. Even members of the professional classes rented from a landlord. The more affluent tradesmen looking for somewhere to invest their money might buy a few houses or even a whole street of sitting tenants. So the idea of buying a house was not necessarily the average couple's first thought in 1950. Since private builders were restricted as to the number of houses they could build for sale, which might in turn be rented out, it fell to the local authorities to provide homes for their area. In some parts of the country council houses had been depleted too by the bombing, so there was already a waiting list for replacements. Until a proper building programme could get under way and produce the required numbers, temporary measures were put into place. These included the revolutionary idea of erecting factory-made prefabricated bungalows.

Renting your home had been traditional in this country for endless generations.

Between 1945 and 1949, including that dreadfully bitter winter of 1947, over 150,000 of these temporary homes sprang up throughout the country, forming new estates. From the outside their lack of traditional brick and slate may have seemed odd but inside they were a revelation! There was a fair-sized living room that had a traditional coal fire with a modern back boiler that not only provided hot water on tap but also wafted warm air into the two bedrooms. There was also a modern bathroom with a heated towel rail. This was everything for which a young family yearned. But it was the kitchen that made most people truly envious. Small and compact, it was modern; everything, including the oven, was built in, but it also had something that was unheard of in the majority of houses at that time – a refrigerator. It was just like a scaled-down version of those kitchens one had seen in American films. With a small garden at the front and a larger one at the back, those tenants who were offered a prefab were considered to be living in the lap of luxury. These buildings were intended to have a limited life; twenty-five years was discussed. However, the photograph shown in the plate section, of part of a road on a large estate started in 1947, was taken in 2011! During their sixty-something years of service the houses have, of course, been renovated and updated but few of their present occupants wish to move.

Somewhat less successful were the 'Airey' houses, again factory made from reinforced concrete columns and slabs, topped with a flat roof. They had the traditional interior layout of a three-bedroom house but, externally, were not only somewhat austere to look at, but over the years developed structural problems. However, they served their purpose for a time, giving the local authorities a breathing space as they set about acquiring more land, often agricultural on the edges of town, in order to start a proper building programme – once restrictions were lifted and supplies became available – of modern, well-designed homes for the post-war generation. In planning these estates, the architects, having looked at the narrow streets of small terraced houses of the past, took the opportunity presented to them of providing plenty of open spaces, using not only front gardens but also wide expanses of grass, often planted with trees, between the pavement and the road. Unfortunately, when the designers drew up their plans for the future, none of them foresaw the expansion of the car industry and so, although they also provided sizeable back gardens, they failed to leave sufficient space between each pair of semi-detached houses for either a parking space or a future garage. Thus it is that sixty years on, in many estates the once beautiful greenswards beyond the pavement are little more than elongated car parks.

To help overcome the housing shortage, those who had a home were encouraged to share theirs with others. Families who, during the war, had had either evacuees or soldiers billeted on them and had finally got their house back to themselves now found it was happening all over again, the only difference being that at least they were allowed to choose with whom they would share. Very few of the brides who married in the first few years of the 1950s went straight into a house of their own. Often, a girl coming back from her honeymoon found herself returning to her old bedroom. The only difference was that now she had to share that room with her new husband. If the family home was large enough or there were no other children occupying a bedroom, then it might be possible for her parents to let the couple have the use of another room as a sitting room.

> We shared with my stepmother, two sisters and two half brothers, but we did buy our own bedroom suite.
>
> Dot, Ipswich

> We had two rooms in my parents' house, one of which we furnished with a full dining suite bought second hand from a school friend who had never used it. Plus a Utility settee and two chairs. I cooked the evening meal for the two of us when I got home from work. I had to fit in with my mother when it came to things like doing our washing.
>
> Mary, Birmingham

> We moved into a large caravan, like a mobile home. Most of the furniture was fitted or given to us.
>
> Mabel, Cumbria

All these ladies married in the early 1950s, but the availability of affordable housing either to rent or buy was still difficult in 1956.

> Our first home was in an old lady's house in Barnet. The minister of the church we attended recommended us to her. The house was a suburban three bedroom semi. We had the front room downstairs which had her furniture and the back bedroom. Her previous tenants had had their own bedroom suite so she asked us to do the same. As it happened my in-laws had given us a bedroom suite for a wedding present. I remember it was quite a job getting the wardrobe up the stairs. We shared the kitchen and bathroom which wasn't really a problem but the old lady was obviously very lonely, so we saw quite a bit of her.
>
> Mollie, Suffolk

There were problems for both parties in any of the arrangements but especially for the bride. If the couple were living with her parents then, as far as they were concerned, she was still their 'little girl' and, consequently, they would often interfere or make suggestions on how she should do things. For her new husband, although he was out at work all day, he could not feel truly at home in a place where previously he had been a guest. Then there were practical matters about such things as times for the use of the bathroom and kitchen. Mother might hint that it was much easier for her to cook meals for them all, or if she did allow her daughter the use of the kitchen there could be problems over the storage of personal food supplies, dishes left unwashed and sinks not cleaned, all of which could lead to tension if not rows between them all. It could be worse if the couple moved in with the husband's family. Unless the new wife had earlier established a good rapport with her new mother-in-law she could very quickly be made aware of her shortcomings, whether it be her inability to cook 'proper meals' or her failure to iron her husband's shirts as they should be done. By and large, it was probably better to steer clear of either parental home and opt to live with a stranger, even if it meant paying much more rent.

Many couples spent up to two years living with their family or in lodgings, often having their first baby in these cramped conditions. Those who had their names on their Local Authority Council Housing List found that it was not simply a question of moving automatically up the list as the one at the top was housed. Each couple was assessed on a points system. Priority was given to those in essential services – doctors, nurses, midwives, firemen and policemen too if the local police force had insufficient housing stock of its own. Then came the families in greatest need. Some authorities insisted that to get a step towards the top of the list a couple had to have two children, an incentive that further increased the already rapidly rising birth rate. Harsh though it sounds, one couple who were promised a house on the strength of a forthcoming second child were put on hold when it was discovered that the infant might be a 'blue baby' and thus might not survive. Fortunately she did, and her parents were able to move out of the two rooms they rented in an austere box-like bungalow to an almost brand-new council house.

It was a red-letter day when a couple were finally informed they had been allocated a house. However, in those parts of the country where the need was greatest, there could be a small snag – they were still expected to share it, this time with another young couple! In Dot's case she and her husband and baby daughter were allocated the upstairs of a house, which gave them two reasonable-sized rooms with the third small bedroom for the baby. They had the advantage of having the bathroom on their floor but it had to be shared with the childless couple downstairs who had, in house agent's parlance, the two reception rooms. Again the kitchen was shared but the ground floor tenants also had access to the outside lavatory. Fortunately Dot did not have to share for long and she still remembers that wonderful day in March 1955:

It was brand new. The house was finished but nothing else was! The road hadn't been made up and there was no garden as such. Being winter there was mud everywhere and the house itself was so damp. The Council were so anxious to get people into homes that they didn't allow time for the houses to dry out properly. For the first few weeks we lived downstairs, which we could heat, in an effort to get rid of the damp. But at last we had a place of our own.

4

Making It Like Home

Young people starting to furnish a home today are governed by how much they can afford, either in actual cash or on their credit cards. In the early 1950s, apart from money the major consideration was the dreaded 'dockets' or units. Like everything else during and immediately after the war, new furniture was rationed. Because of the shortage of imported wood, selected furniture manufacturers throughout the country had been required to produce goods made from home-grown supplies. This was known as utility furniture, and it carried the insignia of two capital Cs and a 41: CC41. Units to be used when buying furniture were initially limited to those who had lost their homes through the bombing or were recently married and were setting up home for the first time. If the marriage was called off before the actual ceremony took place then the units had to be handed back. The maximum allocation was sixty units with another ten for each child. A large wooden item such as a wardrobe was twelve units, a 4ft bedstead five, a dining table six, a complete kitchen cabinet eight – if you were running short then you might have the bottom cabinet for five and dispense with the top that required three more. The government leaflet containing these figures has in bold type: 'No allowance can be made for lodgers or visitors.' Bearing in mind that furniture included such things as cots, high chairs and playpens, all requiring precious 'dockets', it is not surprising that there was a brisk trade in second-hand furniture. Recycling was at its peak as young couples happily accepted the unfashionable but no longer wanted items of friends and family or trawled through the contents of second-hand shops to find pieces that they could use. A coat of paint here, a good polish there and many redundant chests of drawers, washstands and old-fashioned wardrobes were given a new lease of life. If the last mentioned item happened to be the sort where the clothes cupboard usually sat atop a long deep drawer, then the two could be parted and, if necessary, the drawer might find an entirely new use as a baby's first cradle.

However, by the time we get to the second half of the decade, restrictions were lifted, the furniture industry was in full swing, and, moreover, private builders were building houses for sale. These too tended to be large estates of either small bungalows or semi-detached houses. Again, many were built without garages or the space for one, but the back garden would allow room for a shed to house the family's bicycles, garden tools and possibly also the wringer that came out on washday.

Most couples furnished their homes in the traditional way set by their parents. D., in her meticulously kept little notebook of 1956 labelled 'Wedding', recorded not only the items she purchased for her trousseau and the gifts she and her husband received but, more tellingly, the items they would require to equip the main rooms in their new home. In the bedroom the first item was, of course, the bed. At that

When it came to tucking in the bottom corners of both sheets and blankets, the method used in hospital was recommended.

time many beds still consisted of a heavy iron frame with wooden head and foot boards supporting a base made of coiled springs or tightly woven mesh. On this was laid the mattress. The thick feather mattress had mostly fallen into disuse except for children and the elderly, most people having what were known as flock mattresses. The outer covering of strong cotton fabric, often printed in blue or red stripes, was stuffed with waste wool and other materials. To ensure overall evenness the flock was secured firmly in place at regular intervals with circular discs of tufted thread which went right through the mattress. The drawback to these mattresses was that after years of wear the flock matted into uncomfortable lumps and the tufted discs either came out or else caused discomfort. The early forms of interior sprung mattresses also had their drawbacks when, for some reason, one of the metal springs unravelled and poked through the mattress, perhaps giving the sleeper a nasty scratch. The firm of Slumberland, which had developed their interior sprung mattress in the 1930s, had their production severely curtailed by the war, but by the early 1960s they were leading the way to a revolution in the bed industry. In much the same way, there has been a major change in what goes on a bed.

In the 1950s most people covered the mattress with either a flannelette sheet or an old blanket; D. was not specific on this, merely writing '1 under blanket'. Over this was placed the bottom sheet, the edges of which were tucked in all the way round the mattress. Then came the top sheet, which was tucked in at the bottom and sides. Sheets were usually sold in pairs marked either single or double size. D. decided three pairs of doubles were sufficient. Sheets and pillowcases were invariably made of cotton and their quality, which depended on whether the cotton had come from Egypt or India, varied from very fine through to the very strong twill which took some getting used to, especially if an economical housewife had turned the sheet 'sides to middle' which, while moving the worn part to the edge of the sheet, left the joining seam right where one usually slept. Next came the woollen blankets which, more than likely, had been made in Whitney. These again were pretty universal: unbleached with possibly a couple of dyed blue or green stripes at each end. One blanket was usual for summer use, two in winter. D. chose not only '2 blankets' but another more modern, lightweight cellular one. When it came to tucking in the bottom corners of both sheets and blankets, the method used in hospital was recommended. With the edges of the top sheet folded over the blankets, the whole effect was one of precise neatness. Next came the eiderdown. This, as its name suggests, should have been made of down but, unless one had paid a lot for it, it was more likely to have been filled with the feathers of a chicken than those of the eider duck. Eiderdowns could be covered with prettily patterned cotton fabric or, more often than not, had the upper side in a silk or satin material in a good, strong, plain colour, rose pink and gold being very popular. The problem with these was that they were not washable and had to be dry-cleaned. In the 1950s the bedding department of many large stores did a steady trade in the refurbishment of old eiderdowns.

D. required four pillows for which she decided she needed eight top pillowcases and twelve under ones. She was allocating two pillows apiece for her and her husband, and therefore dispensing with the bolster that her parents most certainly would have had on their double bed. This was an elongated firm pillow that stretched right across the bed, acting as a base for the soft feather pillows. Large bolster cases were available, similar to the plain white 'housewife' pillowcases. Bolsters were eventually deemed old-fashioned but, ironically, sixty years on, advertisements for them have started appearing in those magazines which contain all those items you never knew you wanted, alongside those that make you say, 'now that's a good idea'. Finally, a bedspread or quilt, a single sheet of material that matched the eiderdown, may have covered the made bed. At night the quilt was removed and every morning on rising the bedclothes were folded back over the foot of the bed to allow it to be aired before being remade after one had breakfasted. It was a slatternly housewife indeed who left her bed unmade throughout the day.

In passing we should mention that, like so much else, bed sizes have changed. The most common size for a double bed was a width of 4ft. The more affluent had the larger 4ft 6in. Children's beds were likely to be either 2ft 6in or 3ft; the latter would comfortably accommodate two children.

As for the rest of the bedroom, a double wardrobe was standard, with, if one could afford it, an additional, smaller, gentleman's wardrobe. Gone, however, was the washstand. With a bathroom in the house there was no longer any need for the china basin and water jug which stood on the marble top, anymore than one would dream of storing the matching chamber pot in the cupboard beneath. All these 'old-fashioned' articles were dispensed with; sold for next to nothing to second-hand dealers who sold them on to eager American tourists! The discarded washstands themselves were stripped of their marble tops and re-covered with a wooden top to re-emerge as small sideboards. There would, however, be a dressing table with either a single or triple mirror and possibly a chest of drawers or tallboy – an interesting piece which had two or perhaps three drawers at the bottom with a two-door cabinet above. These were to prove very chic and useful a few years later for housing a television set, or, in some cases, as a cocktail cabinet – but we're straying now into the 1960s. Flooring throughout the house was likely to be a form of linoleum, which in the bedroom was covered with a rug on either side of the bed. D. hopefully put 'rug or carpet' on her list.

Downstairs, the front room would eventually hold the three-piece suite of sofa and two armchairs, with other luxury items following when the couple could afford them. For many, the dining room was still considered the family living room, with the matching dining set of sideboard, table and four chairs. Two fireside armchairs, straight backed and with wooden arms, were placed where their name implied they should be. In the recesses beside the fireplace might stand the radiogram or a small table with the wireless on top and perhaps a standard lamp. On the other side might be a tea trolley, on the shelves of which would be kept magazines, and the housewife's sewing basket or knitting bag. Shelves at head height might also be fitted into the alcoves to serve as a bookcase or to display ornaments. The top of the sideboard almost always had the wedding-present clock as well as any pieces of wedding-present silver.

Of all the pieces of furniture, the 1950s designers seem to have had most fun with sideboards. These ranged from narrow cupboards either side of two thin drawers, supported on tall spindly legs or a slightly deeper four-cupboard version, again perched on thin legs, to the more solid, more compact, but deeper two or three central drawers with shelved cupboards on either side. Tables were also minimalist in design, a flat square top with hidden pull-out extensions on opposite ends and thin straight legs coming straight from each corner. The chairs were similar in having thin legs and thin bars across the back. The light wood of the home-grown beech was a popular material of the time. More robust in design was the much sought after G Plan, which was considered very modern and not only offered dining sets but three-piece lounge suites that were nothing like those that had been known in recent times. These were all solid wood, with loose, tie-on pads for seating, quite unlike the old-fashioned suites upholstered in uncut moquette. One couple reported that they used their pre-5 April marriage tax rebate to buy their G Plan sofa and two matching armchairs. A couple who had one of these suites was well in the vanguard of fashion. And although fashions have changed over the years, those 1950s suites have held their own, not least because, compared to huge sofas, they are easy to move.

Perhaps the biggest change from the 1950s has occurred in the design of the kitchen. From the Industrial Revolution to the 1930s, the kitchen had been the smallest room in the house, often seeming to be an afterthought to the main building. Even in larger Victorian and Edwardian houses, there was a small scullery where food was prepared and the washing up done, while the actual cooking was done on a coal-fired range in what later became known as the breakfast room. In the two-up, two-down house, the tiny kitchen/scullery often contained a built-in stone copper in one corner in which water was heated on washday and to fill the tin bath on bath night – usually Saturday – and even, recalling Dickens's *Christmas Carol*, to boil puddings. Cooking was done on the fire in the living room, and was often limited to what could be cooked in a saucepan or frying pan, though some fire grates incorporated a small oven to one side of the fire.

In the scullery or back kitchen, unless one was very fortunate to possess what was known as a butler's deep white sink, the standard was a very shallow one made of 'dried-on mustard' yellow stoneware, the outside of which carried a pattern of indentations in which grime could collect. In many families all forms of washing revolved around this sink, from personal ablutions and the weekly laundry to washing up after each meal. For each of these operations a bowl was placed inside the sink; originally it would have been an enamel one but by the 1950s was more likely to be made of plastic. In the days before liquid detergents were generally available, the housewife would have added a handful of household washing soda to the water before washing the dishes. For those who did not have hot water on tap, it was important to follow the old rules of washing up, that is, start with the cleanest objects like glassware and work through to the dirtiest and greasiest dishes and pans. While all were left to drain on the wooden draining board (although sometimes plates would be drained in a rack above the sink), it was usual to rinse glassware in clean cold water before drying and polishing. The inside of the standard yellow sink was very difficult to clean, especially when tea-stained. Invariably, in one corner stood a triangular-shaped strainer into which was tipped, at least three times a day, the leaves from the teapot. Added to throughout the day were vegetable peelings, especially potatoes, and occasional eggshells. At the end of the day the contents of the strainer were put on the living room fire to damp it down and keep it smouldering overnight, so that it could be brought to life again in the morning to boil a kettle for the breakfast cup of tea.

Before I am accused of wandering away from the 1950s, I need to assure the reader that there were many homes throughout the country, particularly in rural areas, where these conditions existed; for many a young housewife of the 1950s this was normal, everyday living. Similarly, there were still houses in towns without electricity where the occupants relied on gas for lighting as well as cooking. Those rural areas that were without either utility had to rely on paraffin oil lamps for lighting and either coal-fired stoves or cookers that ran on bottled gas. Although there were very few town dwellings that were not connected to water mains and sewerage – though not necessarily with a lavatory indoors – the same cannot be said for all country dwellings; many of those living in the country still had to draw their water from a well or a pump and use either an earth or chemical closet housed in a shed in the garden.

Cooking was done on the fire in the living room, and was often limited to what could be cooked in a saucepan or frying pan.

The new builds of the post-war period were of a different shape to houses of the Victorian and Edwardian eras. Instead of the thin rectangle with a half-rectangle extension we now had the totally rectangular house. A pretty standard design had the kitchen and the dining room stretching right across the back of the house with, in many cases, the kitchen larger than the dining room, which in turn was often separated from the sitting room by double glass doors rather than a wall. It would not be long before the separate dining room would give way to the L-shaped living room.

These new, larger kitchens still followed the traditional pattern of placing the sink under the window. At last deep white sinks replaced the horrible yellow ones, and in the early part of the 1950s wooden draining boards would be either side of the sink, each supported on a metal framework. Connections were provided for either gas or electric ovens which, once manufacturers were free to produce new designs, were a world away from the heavy black gas stoves or the blue mottled electric ovens of the past, both of which took up room. At this stage, a walk-in larder, or at least a large cupboard would have been part of the design so there was storage space. That, with a table and a couple of kitchen chairs, was that as far as the kitchen was concerned. No built-in units yet. A curtain in front of the sink framework hid buckets and cleaning materials, saucepans and possibly the Burco boiler – of which more later. But the item which most couples purchased, as soon as they could afford it, was the kitchen cabinet. Painted green, this had two round or oval frosted glass panels in the top cupboard in which one stored dry goods ready to use when cooking. Then came the enamel-covered fold-down flap on which you prepared your pastry and so on. Previously all baking had been carried out on the kitchen table – a plain wooden surface that could be scrubbed after use. But the modern kitchen cabinet provided the equivalent of the 1950s work surface, though, of course, that terminology had yet to be coined for the kitchen. One of the exciting things about this cabinet was the incorporated flour holder which, theoretically, should have emptied out its contents on to the enamel board. Another feature was the small, circular, mesh-covered disc in the doors, which allowed fresh air to circulate within the cupboard. The base of the cabinet held two further storage cupboards.

The idea that one day they would be able to afford a refrigerator hardly ever crossed the mind of the average housewife at the beginning of the 1950s. She had, of course, seen that they appeared to be standard in the American homes depicted on the cinema screen but she knew that anything similar was far too big for a kitchen like hers. However, by the end of the decade, small fridges were available. But until that day came, our housewives continued to do as their mothers had done, buying fresh food daily and using a 'meat safe', preferably in a cold larder, to keep meat fresh and away from flies.

These little wooden box cupboards had a door that was simply a frame to which a heavy-duty mesh was nailed on the inside, through which air could circulate but no creepy crawlies could enter. Here one kept the joint before it was cooked and its remains afterwards, ready to be used cold or minced up for the following day's meal.

A passing thought. All meat safes, like those kitchen cabinets, were painted in pale green. Why was that? Was it that the colour suggested modernity and cleanliness, or that manufacturers found green paint easy to mix? Was there, perhaps, a surplus of that colour? Or was this, as has been suggested, the green paint left over from the war, which, when applied to a piece of wood that stood in the local air-raid warden's front garden, was supposed to turn yellow in the event of a gas attack?

It is to D. that we turn again to discover what she hoped for in her 1956 kitchen. Top of the list was a cooker. She did not specify if this was to be gas or electric. That was followed by a table and two chairs and matting for the floor. More than halfway down the list were a Hoover, a refrigerator and a washing machine; the last did not receive a tick against it, so presumably she had to wait for that. More down to earth was the electric kettle, while showing something of her lifestyle was the coffee percolator. Mundane items include a washing-up bowl, bucket, dustbin, scrubbing brush, pan scourer, dish mop, dishcloth, tea towels and so on. Surprisingly, there is even that ubiquitous sink tidy. She also listed essential items such as a bread bin and a flour bin, as well as all the named storage tins and baking tins, thus indicating that she fully intended to be a 'real housewife' who would be cooking proper meals. The makers of many of the kitchen gadgets she mentioned will be as familiar to the modern reader as they were to the 1950s housewife; one such mentioned was a Prestige egg whisk, as well as their general purpose knife and kitchen set. But she also wanted another innovation of the period: Phoenix ovenproof glass casserole dishes and plates. Phoenix ware was made by a British company as opposed to the better known Pyrex, which was American. Both introduced oven-to-table dishes, but while Pyrex was clear glass, Phoenix offered colourful decorative designs on their plates and dishes.

The espresso coffee bars that arrived in major cities in the mid-1950s introduced the public to the use of both heatproof glass cups and saucers as well as the very colourful sheets of Formica that covered tabletops and counters. Manufacturers began producing more and more small kitchen tables covered with bright blue or yellow Formica and it wasn't long before the material was in great demand for what became the beginning of the fitted kitchen. Once the white sink had been replaced by the moulded enamel sink and draining board that was fitted into a wooden unit that housed under-sink cupboards, it was not long before shops were selling whitewood wall and floor cupboards for the homemaker to install and paint to his or her own taste. By the very end of the 1950s, house builders were beginning to realise that the fitted kitchen was what the public wanted.

In the meantime, it was a question of DIY for those who wanted to get ahead of fashion. In this, magazines played a very large part. One of the criticisms often levelled at life in the 1950s was that the stereotypes of male and female roles were reinforced, in particular in children's books where little girls, always depicted wearing a frilly apron, helped Mummy to do household chores while little boys helped Daddy in the garden or tool shed, perhaps mending a puncture to a bicycle. However, a well-known women's magazine shows a different picture. In a series of articles subtitled 'Save money and enjoy yourself', it promised that the series would help 'to make your kitchen your pride and joy'. One article was dedicated to flooring the kitchen. In the days before lino tiles were available, it was suggested that you could make your own quite cheaply. Having first measured the area of your floor ('turning it into square feet by multiplying the width by the length'), you then needed to buy about four offcuts of lino in different colours. Black, green, red and white were suggested. These were then cut into different sized squares and a patchwork design created. Clear, full details for the whole operation were given, accompanied by photographs of the various stages. What is interesting about these illustrations is that it was a collaborative effort; the young couple were to share the work between them and there was not a frilly apron in sight, the young woman being sensibly dressed in slacks and a sweater.

Having achieved a new floor, the following week's lesson was how to make a useful double cupboard to stand next to the cooker, which would also utilise those awkward few inches left in the corner by including a rounded projection of two open shelves. The whole unit was then topped by a continuous sheet of Formica. What a sense of achievement our housewife and her husband must have had when they had carried out their renovations. It may have taken them longer than having units or a new kitchen floor fitted by a professional, but it would most certainly have cost them much less, and, given that they managed to overcome any stress or strain that the projects created, they could congratulate themselves, if you will forgive the pun, on having further cemented their relationship.

Many of the basic requirements of a home were given as wedding presents. When things were still tight in the early 1950s many brides found that they were given items that had rarely if ever been used by the donor. Often these were silver or silver-plated items of cutlery such as coffee spoons with the distinctive coffee bean design in assorted colours at the end of the long, thin handle. These, like the fluted-bowl fruit spoons or the oddly shaped cake forks, were always presented in a velvet-lined case. The use for many of these items was no longer fashionable, in particular those heavy fish knives and forks which came with ivory or bone handles and were accompanied by the pair of matching servers. Redolent of days long gone and a serving dish with a whole salmon, there was no place for them in the home where husband and wife sat down to a herring or a portion of cod each. Young Mr and Mrs 1950s wanted modern cutlery to suit their modern dining table. In this they were not disappointed. Manufacturers produced stainless steel as well as EPNS tableware in slim, elegant styles, light in weight and often much smaller in comparison to that of the previous generation. Out went the heavy, long-bladed knives with square bone handles and large forks. The steel knives that needed careful cleaning and sharpening (often done on the smooth stone step at the back door) were banished forever while the ancient horn-handled carving set came out only at Christmas: one of the ever-sharp Prestige kitchen knives being much more useful.

Stainless steel came in a variety of grades and consequently the cutlery varied from very cheap to very expensive; the former was

There was not a frilly apron in sight, the young woman being sensibly dressed in slacks and a sweater.

thin and a bit tinny, whereas the most expensive could at a glance be taken for silver. If, however, the 1950s housewife yearned for silver rather than stainless steel, then she was helped in achieving her desire by probably one of the best advertising gimmicks of all time. In the middle of the 1950s Kelloggs launched their Insignia Plate cutlery offer. On each of their cereal packets was printed a token of different value according to the size of the packet. What started with an offer for six EPNS teaspoons for just a small payment plus a certain number of tokens, developed in time into the full range of cutlery. At a price one could afford and over a long period of time it was possible to have a complete table setting for six, including fish knives and forks, and, unlike most canteens of expensive cutlery that contained only two tablespoons, one could purchase six, if one wished. The elegant, somewhat classical, design was pleasing to the eye and each piece carried a twenty-five-year guarantee. As one who made use of this offer from Kelloggs, I can testify that most of it was in constant use for much longer than twenty-five years.

The other large item often given as a wedding present was the dinner service. Mothers-in-law often saw it as their prerogative to purchase the 'best' china for the newlyweds. Those who could afford it felt that there should be a matching dinner, tea and coffee set. Inevitably they would lean towards the makers and designs that had been popular in their own youth, or perhaps what they had hoped for and never had. It took Mollie, for example, a great deal of tact to steer her future mother-in-law away from the heavily patterned Crown Derby fine china towards the modern pottery of Midwinter and her choice of their 'falling leaves' design.

Nearly sixty years on what's left of this much-used tea and dinner set still pleases with its freshness and modernity. The range of interesting shapes and use of unusual colours for crockery in some ways harked back to the designs of the 1920s and '30s, but to a generation which had grown up with a jumble of plates and so on left over from that time, mixed with even earlier ones either handed down or bought second hand and supplemented by the very plain utilitarian replacements available in wartime, these new pieces brought the promise of better times ahead. Midwinter probably produced most of the tableware bought in the 1950s, some of it being within an affordable price range. The coffee pot bearing the large sunflower was very popular, as was its design that moved right away from the traditional-shaped pot with the long curved spout. Other potteries like Poole and Denby produced larger cups and chunkier plates in unusual colours, sometimes combining two bold colours in a cup, the paler of the two on the inside. The sets produced by both these firms were comparatively expensive but it was possible to buy each piece individually. There was, it seems, a desire to return to more natural materials in some cases, one manufacturer opting for very heavy earthenware with the rim of each plate revealing the basic terracotta clay while the main piece was fired with a strong blue glaze with white spots. This surely was intended for everyday use; perhaps it was considered more masculine, but it was unlikely to impress your more aspiring friends.

If you were entertaining some of those to supper, then it was likely that you would offer them a cup of coffee at the end of the meal. Among the gadgets now on sale again were coffee grinders, both the old-fashioned type turned by hand and the modern electric ones, which often came as part of a set with a liquidiser. If you couldn't grind your own coffee beans then, should you have a Kardomah or shop of that ilk in your town, you would buy a packet of ready-ground. Failing that, your grocer would probably stock the very recognisable green tin of Lyons' ground coffee that came in a vacuum pack. It would be well into the 1960s before instant coffee made its appearance. As for preparing the coffee, this could be done in an aluminium or enamel percolator that was heated on the oven hob, or a shiny chromium electric model you could plug in anywhere. If the worse came to the worst then you resorted to boiling it in a saucepan. However, you could use your very modern matching pottery coffee set. One of the mysteries of the 1950s I have been unable to solve is who actually served their guests coffee in demi-tasse cups. These thimble-like cups held at the most half a dozen sips, yet they must have been very popular. Either that or there was a glut in the market at the time and they were sold off relatively cheaply. How else to explain why several people reported receiving as many as four sets each as wedding gifts!

From the modern pottery and dinky demi-tasse to the ultra-modern plastic, which made it possible to equip your home with everything from a cup and saucer right through the range of tableware down to the matching egg cups, cruet set and jam pot. In bright colours and interesting shapes, plastic provided the housewife with the opportunity to choose between the rigid Melamine and the much lighter and less expensive plastic. The products that traded under the name of Melamine, Melaware or Gaydon were reputed to be so tough as to be unbreakable. There was no doubt that on a dark winter's morning it must have been a pleasure to sit down to eat one's breakfast from a turquoise or orange cereal bowl, bacon and eggs from a dark blue plate and tea from a bright red cup with a handle moulded from the rim. But it was the tea cups that led to the eventual relegation of plastic tableware to the picnic basket or camping gear. The inner lining of the plastic cup was white and after a time the tannin in tea stained it very badly. A reliable source relates that when, as a student, she spent a summer working in a holiday camp where Melamine had entirely replaced all the crockery, after the evening meal all the cups were left to soak in bleach overnight. At home an application of Vim would in time roughen the surface of the lining. But for a while plastic ruled, so much so, in fact, that the firm Midwinter actually produced its own version.

It wasn't long before the United States would influence the British housewife yet again, this time taking over the kitchen with the now well-known Tupperware. Whatever anyone may have thought to the contrary, plastic in its many guises was here to stay.

5

The Daily Routine

Most young women who had worked before they married took it for granted that they would continue to do so until such time as they started a family. In the meantime, their wages could be saved towards buying all they would need to set up home when they finally got that longed-for house. Realistically, for those who were living in two rooms in someone else's home, there would have been little to keep a young woman occupied throughout the day had she given up work.

The day started with her preparing breakfast for herself and her husband while he used the bathroom. By the end of the decade she was almost certain to send her man to work on a bowl of cereal, followed by something cooked, like bacon and egg. She might also make packed lunches for them both to take to work should they work in places which did not provide a canteen. After her husband had left, to walk, cycle or to catch public transport to his place of work, our young housewife would have washed up, leaving the kitchen tidy, and then made the bed. If they had one she cleaned the grate and laid the fire ready for the evening before dusting the living room. If she had time she might also put any washing she had in to soak or even begin preparations for the evening meal. Then she could get herself ready for work. As she made her journey to her workplace she might be deciding what she would be cooking that evening for their supper. And cooking it she would be, in those pre-ready-made meals, pre-microwave oven days when the only takeaway meal choice was fish and chips.

Most girls had some knowledge of basic cookery. Some had acquired it almost by a process of osmosis simply by watching their mothers who, as if by magic, never weighed anything but still produced excellent sponge cakes, pastry for pies and delicious suet puddings. The young child who was given the pastry trimmings and a handful of currants or a spoonful of jam to turn into their own creations grew up ready to experiment. In large families it was taken for granted that the children would help with food preparation, starting with peeling vegetables and progressing to the actual cooking until, by their early teens, they were capable of producing a whole meal. In addition, most girls also received domestic science lessons at school. These gave practical instruction on how to make good pastry for pies, batters for pancakes and toad-in-the-hole, how to cook rice and semolina for puddings and included basic cake making, usually in the form of buns. Instruction in the cooking of meat and fish dishes tended to be theoretical, with perhaps the exception of that standby, shepherd's pie. Young ladies from a more affluent background often finished off their scholastic education by attending residential courses in home economics, which specialised in the fine cookery that might be required for the entertainment of one's future husband's dinner guests.

A further, often unrecognised, contributor to a girl's cooking skills was the Girl Guides. We may now laugh at having made 'dampers' over the campfire, but any Guide attending camp in the 1950s was expected to take her turn with her patrol at providing the daily meals for the rest of the company. These would include porridge for breakfast – put in the large billycans to soak overnight – stews with vegetables, custard to accompany the blackberries picked from the surrounding hedgerows and then stewed, and even, when the weather turned sultry and the milk turned sour, making cream cheese by suspending it in a muslin bag from the branch of a tree. But the Guide movement's input into a girl's domestic education was not limited to the campsite. During the rest of the year a Guide was encouraged to study for the Cookery, Laundress, Homemaker and Hostess badges, all of which gave her valuable experience she would carry with her for life.

Unless our young woman actually worked in the town centre, her daily shopping was likely to be from the shops she passed to and from work. In the 1950s most areas had their own parade of local shops, which would have included a post office, butcher, greengrocer, grocer, newsagent, baker and dairy. In many places there would also have been a fishmonger, possibly a fried fish shop, and invariably a draper who also sold knitting wool, and a chemist. In fact, everything one needed. Many of these were individually owned, family-run businesses, with only the occasional one that was part of a chain such as the Express Dairy, where in parts of London it was possible to buy flavoured yoghurt in small glass jars. This new commercially produced 'foreign' food had only been found before in its natural state in delicatessen stores. It would be some years before both yoghurt and delicatessen counters or shops found their way into shops outside the capital.

The young child who was given the pastry trimmings and a handful of currants or a spoonful of jam to turn into their own creations grew up ready to experiment.

Most of the previously mentioned shops were to be found in villages too, if not separately, as shop buildings sometimes combined two or more; for example a butcher's on one side and a grocer's on the other. Newspapers and sweets could be found at the post office, while a general store stocked everything from vinegar drawn from the barrel to paraffin, puncture-repair kits and cycle tyres, Wellington boots and those famous candles depicted in that well-loved Two Ronnies' sketch. For a picture of what the general shop, or corner store as it was sometimes known, was like in the 1950s, Ronnie Barker's *Open All Hours* comedy is hard to beat. For those living in remote areas there was also the mobile shop, which was happy to order whatever clients needed. Back in urban areas, there was, of course, the mobile service provided by the Co-op, which not only delivered milk to your doorstep, but also bread, fruit and vegetables, meat and coal.

Wartime rationing had tied the housewife to particular shops where her ration books were deposited. This meant fair shares of whatever was available but it also built up strong customer relationships. If a new housewife continued to live at or near her old home, she was most likely to use the shops her mother used. It would take time to break this routine and become more daring in one's shopping habits. But for now, our working young housewife would either shop in her lunch hour if she worked in a town or on her way home. Highly efficient young women like Jean might even leave an order on their way to work for collection on their return in the evening.

In those far-off days of the 1950s it was taken for granted that everyone would have a proper break for an hour, at least, to eat a midday meal. Ronnie Barker's shop, like many corner shops, might have been open all hours, but in the 1950s trading hours were carefully observed and every small shop, along with many offices and factories, actually closed some time between twelve and two o'clock. You would no more think of going to the dentist or visiting your solicitor during the dinner hour than you would expect the butcher to be open. You could call in at the bank but then they were a law unto themselves, closing their doors to business at three o'clock in the afternoon. While on the subject of shop hours, some may be surprised to learn that all shops closed at one o'clock on one day during the week, usually a Wednesday or Thursday. Annoying as this could be if one was unlucky enough to visit a strange town on early closing day, it was intended as compensation for the shopworkers who were expected to work on Saturday afternoon instead. Factory and office workers had a half day on Saturday. Evening closing hours were also strictly enforced in shops and offices, and the idea of Sunday opening, late night or even twenty-four-hour shopping was a totally alien concept. Only certain small shops were allowed to open at different times.

In some areas, men expected to go home at midday to eat a proper cooked dinner, topped off with the inevitable cup of tea, an intrinsic part of the British diet. The working wives of these men would have left a stew or pudding cooking slowly and would probably reach home slightly ahead of their men in order to be ready to dish up as soon as they came in. We talked then of a 'dinner hour' and for many people the main meal of the day was at one o'clock. After an afternoon at work, most folk went home for their tea. This was no longer the 'afternoon tea' of cucumber sandwiches and a cake, but a more substantial meal, something hot, possibly on toast, perhaps with a dessert but always accompanied by tea, drunk from cups on saucers, and poured from a brown glazed pot invariably covered by a knitted or padded tea cosy. For those who did not return home in the middle of the day, their dinner was eaten at teatime, and so evolved the various names we now give our evening meal. Supper for most people meant a very small pre-bedtime snack, often no more than a biscuit and a cup of cocoa. Bread and cheese with pickled onions were eaten at your peril!

So what did our housewife cook? *Good Housekeeping's Popular Cookery*, first published in 1949 and revised in 1958, offers twenty-four recipes for meat dishes starting with Irish Stew, using neck of mutton, Brown Stew, using stewing beef, followed by Mutton Hot-Pot. After these mundane recipes we pass to Fricassée of Veal, Blanquette of Veal and Veal Goulash, reminding us that veal was used far more in those days before intensive rearing methods caused the meat to disappear from most butchers. A Bacon and Butter Bean Casserole featured too, alongside a Liver and Bacon Hot-Pot; Boiled Salt Beef and Dumplings; Stuffed Heart, Tripe and Onions; Fried Sweetbreads; Stewed Oxtail; Boiled Ox Tongue; and, finally, Toad-in-the-Hole. Under the title 'Rechauffeé Dishes' appear five recipes for using up leftovers. The instructions for making Shepherd's Pie are interesting as it does not specify that the leftover minced cold meat should be mutton, thus distinguishing it from Cottage Pie, which used beef. Another sign of the times was that the onions for this dish were fried in dripping. Lard was probably used when frying the rissoles, which also used up cold meat from which 'all skin and gristle was removed' before being finely chopped or passed through the mincing machine. A Baked Meat Loaf could be made with minced cold meat or sausage meat, while a carrot, a turnip and half an onion boiled in water or stock with a bay leaf, parsley and thyme served as the basis of the gravy in which cooked mince was brought to the boil to make a hash. But possibly the most economical of these leftover dishes was Minced Meat and Macaroni:

2 oz. macaroni; ¼ pint stock
½ oz. dripping; 2 oz. minced cold meat
1 chopped onion; 1 tsp. chopped parsley
1 oz. flour; Salt and pepper

Cook the macaroni in boiling salted water for 20–30 minutes until tender, then drain. While the macaroni is cooking, melt the fat, add the onion and fry. Stir in the flour and stock to make a gravy – use gravy browning if necessary to give a good dark colour. Add the cold meat and heat it through. Stir in the cooked macaroni, chopped parsley and seasoning, and serve immediately.

Uncooked macaroni would have been found in most cupboards at that time as it was used not only to make macaroni cheese but also as an alternative to rice in a milk pudding, a great standby for school dinners and much loathed by many pupils. It would be many years before the term 'pasta' would enter our everyday vocabulary to cover the tantalising selection of shapes and sizes of this 'foreign' food.

The more adventurous way to use leftovers was to turn them into a curry, of which there are nine recipes in the book. How today's home cooks, as well as chefs, would laugh to read that every single one uses curry powder in varying measures. There's nothing wrong with using curry powder but at least nowadays we have the option of choosing the strength of the mixture rather than accepting a one-size-fits-all mixture, although, of course, as we all know, it's so much better if one blends one's own spices! Each of these recipes includes an onion and an apple, with the addition perhaps of a few sultanas; one even includes a teaspoonful of 'table sauce' without making it clear if this was brown sauce or Worcestershire.

If our housewife did not wish to prepare a meat dish, she might choose instead to cook fish for her and her husband's evening meal. With well-stocked wet fish shops, as they were known, our young woman, who would have been brought up to eat whatever fish was in season, would have made good use of sprats, herrings, kippers and bloaters, as well as the delicious mixture of the soft and hard herring roes which went so well on toast. Children of the 1950s report that Friday was still the day on which their mothers cooked fish at home.

The young housewife also tried her hand at making puddings and pies for dessert, as well as cakes, buns and tarts. Custard was the usual accompaniment for the sweet, made from a very pale powder with a hint of pink, which miraculously changed into bright yellow when mixed with milk. Reassuringly, Bird's Custard still retains the circular tin of the 1950s even if nowadays it is no longer made of metal. And in those far-off days we all happily used full cream milk. In fact, in most households the cream was taken off for use on breakfast porridge or cereal. Skimmed milk, had it been available, would have brought back memories of the hard times of the 1930s when that was all many mothers could afford to give their young children.

By the late 1950s the shops were offering a much greater selection of foods than had been available during the years of rationing, and food shopping was governed now by price and personal taste. Conservative by nature, the general population was slow to adopt new ideas and it would be amongst the younger generation that experimentation did take place. A late 1950s magazine offered its readers the opportunity to make 'a pastry from the continent. You will like Doboz Torte.' The trendy housewife with time on her hands and sufficient cash to spare might be induced to try this for a special occasion, even though the amounts of some of the ingredients might have shocked her. Did any of those who did try this dare to substitute margarine for the butter? And how many housewives then were really aware of the difference between salted and unsalted butter?

Ingredients
10 oz. of plain flour; A large pinch of salt
10 oz. of butter; 1 oz. of caster sugar; Cold water to mix

For the Filling and the Sides.
3 egg yolks; 6 oz. of granulated sugar
¼ pint of water; 6 oz. of unsalted butter
4 oz. of plain dessert chocolate
2 tablespoonfuls [sic] of strong black coffee
2 oz. of finely chopped walnuts

For the Caramel Top
3 oz. of granulated sugar; 6 tablespoonfuls of water

The directions were, as they always were in magazines of the period, detailed and easy to follow, and the accompanying illustration was mouth-watering. If a housewife could achieve this then there was no reason why she could not attempt the two-tier wedding cake which was featured on a later page in the magazine, with the promise that the directions for icing the cakes would follow in the next issue.

However, it would be well into the 1960s before 'foreign' foods began to catch on and spaghetti, for example, would come in long slim blue packets rather than in small pieces in a tin with either a meat or tomato sauce. On the whole, we were a nation of 'meat and two veg' people and when it boiled down to it fancy food was not for those who ate to live.

6

'Twas on a Monday Morning ...

He had left for work early that morning so I decided to put the washing to soak in the kitchen sink ready to take out when I returned from work. We didn't have a washing machine or even an electric boiler like my mother, so it was a question of washing everything by hand. I put in his underpants and vest and a couple of his shirts and hankies and then the two blouses I'd worn last week, a slip, bra and knickers. I filled up the sink with hot water, stirred in powder, probably Omo, gave it a swish round and then went to get myself dressed. The moment I opened the drawer, I knew what I had done! I had put every pair of knickers I possessed in the wash! It was too late to try and rescue a pair because I had no means of drying them. This was long before the days of tights, so there was nothing for it but to face the world in a state of semi-nakedness. As I walked to work, I felt everyone who passed me must be aware of my predicament. I tried to think if I would pass a shop that sold underwear but the one that might have done hadn't yet opened. By the time I reached school I had to go straight to take the register for my class and then it was into Assembly. It was while we were praying that I had a brain wave! And so it came to pass that during my first lesson, I dispatched a pupil with a note to the PE mistress. I knew that if anyone would have a spare pair of knickers she would. In due course another child delivered me a brown paper parcel, which, of course, I was not free to open until break time when I could escape to the cloakroom. Ever grateful to the colleague who came to my rescue, I hadn't bargained on a pair of navy blue gym knickers retrieved from the Lost Property box. But believe me, I never again put anything into soak without first checking it might still be required for wearing!

We know from our history lessons that personal hygiene in the distant past was such that those with money smothered themselves with perfumes to cover the odours of others while the poor rarely removed their meagre clothing or submitted themselves to soap (which was very expensive) and water. So the population as a whole must have been inured to the manifold smells amongst which they lived. Which raises the question one hardly dare ask, namely, did we all smell in the 1950s? Certainly few of us changed into clean clothes daily. The development of new materials which can stand up to constant washing, as well as those which are machine washable, along with major advances in these new washing machines, has changed our habits. In the days when everyone wore jumpers and pullovers knitted from pure wool, these were items which required very careful washing. If the water was too hot, there was a strong likelihood of shrinking the garment or of it becoming matted. Woollens required careful hand washing with soap flakes rather than the more abrasive powders used for dirtier items, and also needed extra care in the drying process. Water had to be gently squeezed out of them; they needed to be dried flat rather than hung on a line – which could so easily stretch them – and never, ever, put them close to the fire to dry. Small wonder then, that men's thick sweaters in particular did not get washed as frequently as they should have done in those pre-male-deodorant days!

For the majority of stay-at-home housewives in the early 1950s, Monday was still regarded as washday. This was because, with the progress of time, it had become customary for the family to have a bath on Friday or Saturday night (whether one needed it or not, as one young man expressed it) and put on clean clothes for the week ahead. Although baths were rarely taken more than once a week, even in households where there was a bathroom, it was expected that each member of the family would have 'a proper' wash each morning before going off to work or school. This particular ablution was known as a strip wash, though some junior members were likely to forget that they had ears or underarms. The clothes worn during the week were then consigned to the laundry basket ready for Monday's wash.

Beds were stripped of their sheets and pillowcases; in households where bedding was in short supply, only the bottom sheet was changed weekly, the one that had been on the top taking its place on the bottom and a clean one coming in as a top sheet. This helped to lessen wear and tear. It was considered necessary to wash sheets at a very high temperature and, if possible, most housewives preferred to boil them along with other white linens such as tablecloths. Sheets then were made of much stronger and heavier cotton than nowadays and, consequently, double sheets in particular were difficult to deal with. Those who could afford it sent their sheets, pillowcases and table linen to a commercial laundry, which returned them beautifully starched and ironed. Those on a tighter budget had the option of the 'bag wash' – the forerunner of the coin-operated launderettes, which made their appearance in the early 1950s. These huge wonderful machines, which like so much else brought echoes of American life, were very popular, provided you remembered to sort your whites from your colours.

It had become customary for the family to have a bath on Friday or Saturday night (whether one needed it or not ...)

However for the majority, Monday meant lighting a copper, plugging in the electric Burco boiler or filling the sink from the Ascot water heater ready for the washing, which took most of the day. Once the washing had been rinsed thoroughly – and the whites put through an extra rinse that contained Reckitts blue – then the whole lot had to be wrung out to get rid of as much excess water as possible. This process required a very strong wrist action, something that over the years many women developed, but for those that didn't then the wringer or mangle had to be used. Mangles were going out of fashion by then. They consisted of heavy wooden rollers through which the laundry was fed with one hand while the other turned a large circular metal handle. Children were often called upon to help, either by turning the handle or by standing on the other side of the rollers and receiving the material as it came through. A wringer, on the other hand, was a much smaller and more compact 'modern' piece of equipment. Some were small enough to be clamped on to the draining board of the kitchen sink, while those on a stand were more robust. The principle was the same as the mangle only the wringer's rollers were much narrower and covered in rubber, but both could prove very dangerous if fingers were not removed in time when guiding through the wet washing.

Each load of washing was then hung out to dry on a line that straddled either the backyard or garden. When the line was full, a clothes prop – a long piece of wood with a V cut into the top – was slipped into the middle of the line and then elevated so the clothes could happily flap in the wind to dry. That was the theory. In practice, particularly in winter, the clothes were often still wet, or at least damp, when they were brought in. Some kitchens had a wooden drying rack suspended from the ceiling that could be let down; the damp laundry was then placed on it and it was hauled up again, leaving the laundry to dry overnight. Most families also had a clothes horse – not the plastic-covered thin metal, concertina-type airer but a proper wooden bi-fold stand (very handy when inverted for making a tent), which could be placed in front of the fire. Because, of course, in wintertime there would have been a coal fire in the living room and it is also possible that there would have been a large mesh fireguard that went right round the hearth at waist height. The brass top of this provided another convenient ledge on which to hang damp garments. Monday evenings in winter had their own, very special, smell!

There was just one ritual left to complete washday and that was 'the folding of the sheets'. Every child in the past must have served an apprenticeship in the art of holding the corners of sheets and tablecloths, learning not to let go at the wrong moment, how to make the correct folds and when to pull slightly on one side or the other to get them level, until they were ready for the following day when the housewife would do the ironing.

By the 1950s it was only those who lived in rural areas without an electricity supply who were still reliant on the flat iron heated on the fire. The urban dweller would have had an electric iron very similar to those we use nowadays, except, of course, there would not have been any steam irons. Everyone knew that water and electricity was a very dangerous mixture. If one needed to achieve the steam effect while ironing, the trick was to cover the item with a dampened cloth and run the iron gently over it, but one had to be very careful not to get any actual water on the sole plate of the iron as this could result either in a blown fuse or, at worst, the destruction of the iron's element. So one of the things our housewife needed to learn was how to mend a fuse. This was not as easy as it is today. To start with the fuse box was usually in some dark and often almost inaccessible cupboard and, after the main switch had been turned off, it was necessary to open the box and thread the correct-sized fuse wire round the china platelets. The good housewife needed to know exactly where the fuse wire was kept as well as making sure that it was replenished after use.

With the tremendous increase in electrical equipment over the years, it has become necessary for builders to make sure that new housing is provided with sufficient electrical sockets to accommodate it all. But in the 1950s there were a great many older houses that did not have any at all. In many houses the central light fitting provided the power source into the metal holder at the end of the piece of flex into which the light bulb fits. An adaptor made of brass covered with bakelite (an early form of plastic) was inserted. The bulb was then put back and from the side extension another plug was fitted in. This might be for the iron, which would have had a sufficiently long cord to reach the table below and allow movement. When not in use for the iron, the adaptor was frequently used to carry the wire connected to the wireless set. In time, householders had one or two electrical sockets installed, usually close to the fireplace, and these then provided the power for standard lamps, radiograms and the much-sought-after television set.

Having plugged in the iron, our housewife would, in the early part of the 1950s, have ironed on the kitchen or living room table. Some women had a board that they placed upon the table – the leaf of an extending table was often used – covered with an old blanket or some other means of padding and topped with a clean piece of sheeting kept specifically for that purpose. Those wives who had several shirts and blouses to iron may have invested in a small portable wooden block, shaped to take the shoulders and sleeves of such garments. Although shaped heavy wooden ironing boards were available it was a real boon when the modern lightweight metal ironing board was introduced towards the end of the decade.

Then once she had the ironing board it wasn't long before the 1950s housewife dreamed of cutting down on the hard physical labour of washday by owning a washing machine to do the work for her. During her visits to the cinema, the housewife had glimpses of the wonderful laundry aids to be found in American homes. Naively, she believed that these were available in every home, most of which had either a specially designated laundry room or occupied a small corner of the enormous garage that every film-set home possessed. Even those who occupied apartments – they didn't have flats like us – had access to a communal laundry room in the basement of the block. The American housewife also had a huge refrigerator in her deluxe kitchen; although the sensible English housewife realised that these were far too big and expensive for her, she did hanker for that washing machine. Hoover had advertised their machine at the Festival of Britain but it was not until the second half of the 1950s that smaller versions of the American models were being produced in British factories. They were expensive but often the decision to buy one was justified by the arrival of a baby and all the extra washing that would entail.

It wasn't long before the 1950s housewife dreamed of cutting down on the hard physical labour of washday by owning a washing machine.

The English Electric Company introduced their machine in 1955. It was what became known as a top-loader. It was square, often a creamy yellow, had a lid that lifted off – just as the old copper lid had – and contained nothing more than a central revolving paddle. It was filled by connecting a hose to either of the taps on the sink. The machine could heat the water to boiling but obviously if one started off with hot water, this cut down on the time needed to reach the required temperature. Most housewives started off with their boil wash and, as the water cooled, added the more delicate items. This model included a wringer that normally sat at the back of the tub but, when rinsing and wringing took place, could swing out over the sink. When the washing was completed, the hose was hooked over the edge of the sink and the water was pumped out. The next development was the twin tub. Again it was a top-loading machine but instead of being square it had become an oblong with part of the space occupied by the washing area with its paddle, while the slightly smaller portion was a drum, which supplanted the wringer and spun at high speed to remove the water from the laundry. It was a major step forward but it would be at least another ten years or so before the fully automated front-loading machine was introduced and, with it, the revolution in types of detergent.

The bride who became a housewife in 1950 had been brought up not to waste many things including soap. In the five years following the end of the war, soap had remained on ration. Each ration book was allotted four coupons a month, so for the average family of two adults and two children sixteen would have been available. Each coupon represented one of the following: a 4oz bar of hard soap – often used for laundry; a 3oz bar of toilet soap – Lux, Lifebuoy, Pears were popular brands; ½oz of liquid soap; 6oz of soft soap; 3oz of soap flakes – used for hand washing delicate fabrics like woollens and silk; 6oz of soap powder. Anyone who used the launderette in the early days will recall that one could purchase small packets of soap powder for use in the machines. These measured amounts never seemed enough and clients often brought extra with them to supplement the packets. The 1950s housewife would also have grown up accustomed to the huge posters, which used to be posted on bill boards in prominent places, extolling the virtues of Persil, which washed whiter. The child whose mother used Oxydol instead was likely to be made to feel inferior when his shirt was judged alongside that of his classmates. Even in wartime the advertising industry had not run down; in spite of paper rationing magazines still carried advertisements for soaps and soap powders and the most successful piece of advertising aimed at children was surely the slogan 'Tizer, the appetiser, will be back when the war is over', which impacted on those who didn't even know what Tizer was.

7

Putting on the Style

In the same way that people can recall what they were doing when they heard of the shooting of President Kennedy or they saw the first television pictures of the attack on the Twin Towers, so any woman old enough will remember her first sighting of the New Look. After all the years of austerity and restrictions, suddenly here were revolutionary new designs in women's clothes. The emphasis was on the word 'new' yet anyone who knew anything about the past realised that what Dior had done was to take his inspiration from the turn of the century. Instead of the knee-length skirts of the 1940s and the straight-cut suit jackets, hemlines were dropped almost to the ankle, waists were nipped in to resemble those highly corseted 18in ones of late Victorian times, and some designs even attempted a bustle effect. It was all quite mind-boggling – and of course – 'not for us'.

However, it was not long before the couture designs were adapted for the high street and the ankle-length hemline retreated up to the calf. The pencil skirt worn with a neat frilly blouse tucked in at the waist was very popular for young business women while the older woman opted for the complete ensemble of the fitted jacket, which emphasised the waist. The drop in skirt length had an unexpected impact on, of all things, the gymslip worn by schoolgirls. This universal garment, consisting of three box pleats front and back, fastened on the shoulders with buttons and tied round the middle

82

with either a matching belt or a fringed girdle, was supposed to be a regulation length. In most girls' schools a termly inspection involved each class kneeling on the floor of the gymnasium while the PE mistress, armed with a measuring stick, ensured that the gymslip was the requisite 4in off the ground. Woe betide the girl who tried to get away with a longer length by pushing out her chest and tucking up the back! Those wily PE teachers knew all the tricks. But life is all swings and roundabouts; schoolgirls nowadays are berated for shortening their skirts until they resemble a curtain pelmet.

Released from restrictions and geared up for a market ready for change, factories were producing not only a plentiful supply of ready-to-wear clothes for the shops but also the basic materials needed to make them. Rolls of cottons, silk, satin, taffeta and fine woollen cloth now filled the shelves of drapery departments in large stores throughout the country, their producers well aware that they would have a ready market amongst the women of this country who had learned to sew in times of need. Now, instead of having to turn a blanket into a winter coat, there would be the opportunity to buy beautiful tweed to make the coat of one's dreams. And those dreams were fostered by the manufacturers of paper patterns. How many young women whiled away a Saturday afternoon in a department store, leafing through those enormous glossy pattern books produced by Butterick, McCalls, Simplicity and Vogue. Many of our 1950s brides chose their wedding dress design this way and, having chosen a pattern, it was then across to the counter to pick out the material, the thread, the zip or buttons; everything, in fact, that was needed before going home to start cutting out.

This was the period when at last British women could share in the new materials that had been readily available to the American market – materials that had been developed in a chemistry laboratory, often as an offshoot of some other research. The 1950s housewife was familiar with nylon – or at least with the stockings which went by that name – but it would not be long before she would be wearing lingerie and nightwear made of nylon and then sleeping on nylon sheets. It was only a step or two to the introduction of brushed nylon, which, with the emergence of the company known as Brentford Nylons which had a store in most areas of the country, appeared to be taking over the whole domestic scene.

The more one looks at the fashions of the 1950s the more the word 'elegant' comes to mind. It was now possible for everyone to dress well for a reasonable price. Once cotton, for example, had been treated so that it was easy to wash and needed little ironing to retain its freshness, summer dresses in particular were a joy to behold. A young woman who possessed a couple of 'Horrockes' dresses was well set up to go anywhere, and if she was prepared to make her own then she could have more than two. The only problem was deciding which design to choose. By the mid-1950s, these cotton dresses, still calf length with a tightly belted waistline, had billowing skirts supported by either paper nylon or stiffened underskirts.

The more one looks at the fashions of the 1950s the more the word 'elegant' comes to mind.

To complete her outfit, our young 1950s wife would have worn both a hat and gloves when she went out. For summer the hat would have been close fitting: a Juliet-style cap, or a simple stiffened band some 5in or 6in wide in a material that matched or toned with the dress. Both the new queen and her sister, Princess Margaret, were as much fashion leaders to copy as were film actresses like Grace Kelly, Doris Day, Marilyn Monroe, Audrey Hepburn and Leslie Caron. Gloves were considered much more than simply items to keep your hands warm in winter. The 1950s women had been brought up by mothers who considered that 'no lady left the house without her gloves on – not put on as she walked down the street – but put on in the hall before she checked in the hall mirror that she was fit to face the world!' So gloves were worn all the year round. In summer these might be white or light-coloured wrist-length items in nylon or thin cotton or possibly crocheted. If one was attending a special function such as a wedding or garden party, and your outfit had very short sleeves, then one would wear long gloves that stretched beyond the elbow. Long gloves were also worn with evening dresses, which were no longer the prerogative of the upper classes, but featured in the 1950s wardrobe for occasions such as the firm's Christmas dinner dance.

Again it was the women's magazines that came to the young woman's aid in showing her not only what was fashionable but also how she could, with 'a few deft touches give new life to many of the old-timers so that you will enjoy wearing them out instead of feeling bored by their all-too familiar looks'. In 1959, we are told that 'waist lines have swerved from high to low and back again to the middle so it is possible to wear dresses one has had quite a long time. Hemlines too have become shorter, but not too short. The addition of a belt, at least four inches wide, will do great things to bring you up to date.' However, rather than suggesting the reader should go out and buy an expensive belt, directions were given for making your own. Describing how one could give a new lease of life to last year's button-through biscuit-coloured wool dress, it was suggested that a wide bright tangerine belt of stiffened material, or a bought one in patent leather, would transform the dress. Strangely, this same advice was being given in television fashion programmes in 2011, though the modern gurus stopped short of also recommending the tangerine beret and shoulder posy of wired orange berries. Further hints for updating included removing the collar from a suit jacket and changing the neckline into the more fashionable boat shape. At the same time the bottom hem could be turned up to fit just below the waist. If the jacket had a round neck it was suggested that this could be cut more deeply and the jacket could be worn over a high necked jersey. To complete the renovation it was essential to cut off the cuffs, making the sleeves three-quarter length so that they 'will not get in the way at your desk'.

For the women who could afford a new dress for the spring, three patterns were advertised as being available from the magazine for around 2s 9d each. Two were obviously intended for the younger woman: both emphasised the nipped-in waist and billowing skirt. Unlike knitting patterns, these dresses were available in bust sizes from 32in to 40in and required between 4yds to 5yds of 36in-width material, which was a common width for most material at that time. The third design was for the more mature figure and was described as 'being cut on well tried lines' with soft pleats falling from the waist. However, an attempt had been made to make this well-known design more up to date by offering 'a novel feature' – which turned out to be 'an unusual collar through which a gay [that is, a brightly coloured] scarf could be slotted to ring the changes'. This pattern started at bust size 36 and went right up to 48 and needed between 4¼yds to 5¼yds of material. Each of the women modelling these patterns was wearing a hat. The youngest one had an upturned Breton-style straw, the slightly older one sported a version of a hat worn by Grace Kelly, while the mature lady had a close-fitting one in ruched material, possibly to match the colour of her dress. The two younger women wore wrist-length gloves, while the older woman had ones that came halfway between the wrist and elbow.

Of course, our woman did not totter out into the street either barefoot or in her bedroom slippers, for the 1950s witnessed a boom in the shoe industry too. From the sensible court shoe with a 1in to 1½in heel, this was the period of slender high heels and very narrow pointed-toed 'winkle-pickers', as the male version was known. The high heels, surely never quite as high as those of the twenty-first century, reached their apotheosis in the 1960s stiletto heel, a lethal menace with its steel tip, which was the ruination of parquet, lino and wooden floors generally. It was estimated that the weight of the average woman standing on the spot wearing a pair of stiletto heels was the equivalent to that of an elephant! Many women suffered the acute embarrassment of becoming stuck when their heel sank right through someone's precious lino. Yet Mrs and Miss 1950s continued to force their feet into these shiny patent leather shoes, which came in vivid greens, reds and yellows – such a relief after years of black or brown – giving little thought to the corns and bunions they might suffer in later years. Having bought their shoes, a new handbag was needed. No need to go off to somewhere like Salisbury's, which specialised in handbags and umbrellas; the shoe chains like Dolcis carried a display of bags which exactly matched the colour and material of the shoes. Bags at that time tended to be fairly small and compact, either a clutch type or box-like with a small carrying handle. The large shoulder bag would have been too reminiscent of a school satchel or, at worst, a gas mask case, although those who needed to carry a lot with them might choose a leather bucket bag. However the majority of our women did not require a large bag as they carried little beyond a purse and a small make-up pouch, a clean hankie and the door key. No mobile telephone, no chequebook, no car keys, no wallet for credit cards … how did they manage?

Was it in the 1950s that many women gave up wearing vests? Or, put another way, why did they jettison this item of underwear? It can't have been due to central heating, for this had still to come. So was it because a vest really was not a very attractive item of clothing? Pause for a moment and think of some of those racy moments on film when a couple proceed to undress. Can you call to mind the image of the woman taking off her vest? On the other hand, men seem to have clung to their vests, even appearing in them in passionate scenes. The vest was a very utilitarian garment, uninteresting in its basic design and manufactured in some cases in a cotton material known as Locknit. Women did have the option, albeit an expensive one, of choosing a more feminine style made of a fine woollen mixture. This had a camisole top with ribbon shoulder straps and was shaped to the contours of the body, reaching right down to the lower back. The vest, if worn, was put on after the brassiere, or the bra, as it became known in the 1950s, perhaps to avoid confusion with a brasserie, a word not common in most people's vocabulary at the time unless they were in the habit of visiting certain restaurants such as one of Lyons Corner Houses in London. A different emphasis in the pronunciation of brassiere could result in a further confusion with the brazier, the night watchman's bucket of burning coals. A 1950s Latin teacher had to hide her amusement when one of her pupils carefully translated a passage that described how a Roman called Lucius thrust his hand into a fiery burning brassiere!

There was a time when, as one walked along a street, usually of Victorian or Edwardian houses, one might spot a small brass plate situated beside the front door. Beautifully polished each day, these plates contained a finely etched name followed by a series of letters, discreetly advertising that this was the home and workplace of a dental surgeon or a music teacher. But gone is the brass plate that used to state 'Spirella Corsetier'. Inquisitive children who enquired the meaning of these words were usually fobbed off with 'that's nothing to do with you' or worse, 'you don't need to know about such things', which made it all the more intriguing. But, of course, your mother would not have wished to discuss details of such personal items as made-to-measure corsetry. There were already old established drapers' shops which specialised in ladies' lingerie and that also offered made-to-measure corsetry. But the independent Spirella corsetier must have been an early form of franchising. Like so many other companies, Spirella had started in the United States but, in Britain, was established in Letchworth, where suitable ladies were trained in the delicate art of selling as well as measuring clients for foundation garments. They could either work from their own homes or make visits to the client. They themselves wore the company's corsetry and displayed in their own figures the power of the garments to produce a sleek line under one's clothes. Emphasis was laid upon the importance of wearing a correctly fitted brassiere and keeping one's stomach under proper control. Women who had worn corsets during the 1940s believed that their daughters should be corseted too and many a slightly plump girl found herself in her teens being forced into an all-embracing form of pink or peach boned and laced armour plating that was totally embarrassing for the modern schoolgirl, who had not only to change for gym lessons but strip off all her clothes for showers. But not for long! Her mother and aunts might continue to keep the corset makers in business, but young Mrs 1950s was likely to buy her modern underwear over the counter at Marks & Spencer.

It was during the 1950s that the St Michael brand of underwear sold at Marks & Spencer covered the bodies of most of the women in this country. Quickly building up a reputation for well-made, fashionable and inexpensive garments, it became the shop from which young Mrs 1950s bought her nighties and pyjamas, both the thick winter winceyette variety as well as the trendy cotton, short-trouser ones known as baby dolls. Petticoats became known as slips, and bras and knickers offered a choice of the dainty, pretty flimsy ones to the down-to-earth white cotton ones that could be given a good boil. Perhaps it was something to do with their association with the thick navy or green baggy school knickers that, at this time, the word 'knickers' became unfashionable and was replaced with the American 'panty' or briefs. However, here is another example of things coming full circle as the word knickers is again in use, though it came as quite a shock when in recent years one heard men mention that they wore knickers!

Mrs or Miss 1950s also bought her suspender belts in Marks and if she needed to hold in the flab with more support than a suspender belt afforded, then she was offered a lightweight elasticated girdle, or roll-on, which came complete with suspenders, which of course were necessary for holding up your stockings. And so we move to the hosiery counter, where one had a choice of stockings. Strange now to think that stockings were bought according to one's shoe size and that once upon a time the best were made either of silk or nylon and were fashioned on the shape of a leg. The seamed variety had little flashings which indicated they were 'fully fashioned' so the seam fell comfortably into place on the back of the leg. The sheer silk ones, like the early nylons, were easily snagged with a fingernail and there was nothing worse than going somewhere special and discovering that a ladder had appeared in your stocking. First aid treatment consisted of rubbing a dampened piece of soap just under the end of the run in an effort to stop it going any further. A more drastic method was to apply a dab of colourless nail varnish on it. The drawback here was that it could stick the stocking to your leg. If one wanted to emphasise the back seam, one wore the stockings inside out; this was considered to be eye-catching and thus more attractive. Apart from fine silk, there was also rayon, which was slightly more hard-wearing, but the strongest of all was lisle. However, lisle stockings lacked stretchiness and, being the stockings worn by senior girls at school, were promptly rejected by our young housewives, who probably still had memories of that awful gap between the top of the stocking and underwear, especially noticeable when riding a bicycle in wintertime. The idea that one day she would be pulling on an all-in-one nylon garment that resembled a pair of elongated, shapeless bags grafted on to a larger one that came up to her waist would have been quite incomprehensible as well as seen as totally unhygienic. It's odd, when you think about it, that as women became more liberated they should have embraced such a restrictive item of clothing as a pair of tights. Where is the mystery, the allure and the elegance which once surrounded a pair of silk stockings, encapsulated so well in the advertising of the one brand that was etched in the

To emphasise the back seam, one wore the stockings inside out; this was considered to be eye-catching and thus more attractive.

minds of the 1950s woman – Kayser Bondor? The credits list of every theatre programme of the time always carried the words 'stockings by Kayser Bondor'.

With tights and, currently, the return of stockings being reasonably priced, does anyone today even consider mending a ladder? Yet in the 1950s, most women who were handy with a needle would try to repair stockings if they could. One way was to raid another, more badly laddered stocking and carefully draw out the silk or nylon threads from it. With this in a fine needle one could try to pick up the last stitch of the ladder and then carefully weave in and out all the way up to the top in the same way one would pick up a dropped stitch in knitting. For a time it was possible to buy a very fine tool a bit like a crochet hook that would make the operation a little easier. Then some entrepreneur devised a small machine that could produce a professional finish. According to the advertisements, these machines offered the stay-at-home wife the opportunity to make some pocket money by setting herself up in business repairing stockings for members of the public. There is no record as to how successful either the machine or the company itself were.

During the 1940s, trousers had, for many women, become part of their working clothes. These were very different to the smart, well-cut linen trousers that had featured in the years leading up to the war, and that tended to be worn by what was termed 'the smart set'. Newsreel pictures at the cinema showed Mrs Simpson looking elegant in them; betrousered film stars relaxed on board yachts; and in romantic comedies bright young things wore theirs at weekend country-house parties where they drank cocktails. This was far removed from the life of the average working woman and, in a moralistic age, there was still something 'not quite right' about a woman wearing trousers. So although they were considered fashionable in America it took time for slacks to become widely accepted in Britain. Some men who disapproved of the practice actually forbade their wives to wear them. Others would countenance their being worn for leisure activities such as cycling or hiking or for working round the home. Women too were often reluctant to be tempted into trousers even when they saw how attractive one could look in designs which had a high waist, side zips and a flat front panel, which emphasised a slim figure. Jeans did not arrive on the scene until towards the end of the 1950s. Having been made popular by James Dean in *Rebel Without a Cause*, they were adopted by the emerging teen culture, so again, not really the thing for a housewife.

Once the restrictions on materials had been relaxed, designers were able to be more imaginative in the styles of that which was essential to every woman's wardrobe – the winter coat. In those days, this was not an item one bought annually. It was still ingrained in many that one had a 'best coat'; that is, the new one, which was worn on Sundays and for special occasions such as, for example, a visit to London. London was the centre of the fashion world, as far as Brits were concerned, and everyone who lived and worked there, or was encountered in the great shopping areas of Oxford Street and Regent's Street, seemed to be dressed not just smartly but elegantly. Therefore, when one travelled up from anywhere in the rest of the country, one wore one's best coat, hat and gloves, even though one was more than likely to get smuts on the coat from the smoke that poured out of the train's steam engine. However, once your best coat had been cleaned a couple of times, it was time to move it to everyday use and take the plunge and buy a new one for best. The designs of the 1950s varied from the double-breasted, brass-buttoned Cossack style in black, red or navy – most startling of all in white but not practical for day-to-day wear – which was extremely flattering to a slim figure. This coat, worn with a large fur hat, was bound to excite envy as well as comment. More down to earth was the swagger coat, with its very full swing-back and wrap-over buttonless front. A novel aspect of this design was that a matching tie belt was slotted through the small vent on either side of the waist and drawn round to hold the front in place. These coats came in two lengths, one just below the knee, the other ending on the thigh. Colours were either plain vivid reds, blues or greens, or the more startling huge multi-shaded blocks of the sort which nowadays might be found on a picnic rug.

It is one of those mysteries, like the demise of the knitted woollen vest, as to who decrees when an item of apparel is no longer in vogue. Look at 1950s photographs of street scenes in towns throughout the country and, along with the trams and trolleybuses, the bicycles and motorcycles, most men and women will be wearing hats. When, and why, did people stop wearing them? Every man who was demobilised from the armed forces from mid-1945 was automatically issued with a hat along with the rest of his new civilian wardrobe. Dashing too many of them looked in their homburgs and trilbys. The flat cap was also very popular for everyday wear. In the 1950s most towns and cities boasted a branch of Dunn's the hatters where gentlemen would be presented with an array of varying headgear. However, by the 1960s it had become necessary for the shop to include other items of men's wear. It was in the 1950s too that practically every city businessman travelled to and from his office wearing a bowler hat, which, like his furled umbrella, was almost a badge of office. There are those who think that the refusal to wear hats came from those younger men who had gone through their school days forced to wear a cap, followed by their two-year stint in uniform during National Service. And so, gradually, hats became the prerogative of older men and sportsmen.

This does not, however, explain why hats slowly went out of fashion generally for younger women. The 1950s bride almost always included a hat in her going-away outfit and the average woman still wore a hat for church on Sundays, in many cases still hanging on to the old tradition of buying a new one for Easter. Hats were still de rigueur for weddings and funerals, and if one moved in the right social circles then one definitely wore a hat for a luncheon engagement, while a fetching little cocktail hat might be worn for a drinks party. In the 1950s there were not only numerous small shops which specialised in ladies' millinery, but both Marks & Spencer and British Home Stores had counters close to the main entrance where hats for every season and all occasions were not only on display but could be picked up and tried on. There were even hand mirrors so that you could see from every angle how you looked. Many a 1950s woman whiled away a cold or wet Saturday afternoon trying on hats she had no intention of buying while her

Many a 1950s woman whiled away a cold or wet Saturday afternoon trying on hats she had no intention of buying

husband attended the local football match. But she might have been tempted, if the price was right – and it has to be said that hats were not beyond the purse of many. Of course, for the woman who worked, and travelled in all weathers on her bicycle, a hat of some sort was a very necessary item. A knitted helmet type or pixie hood was ideal for winter wear and again magazines came to the rescue with instructions on how to make these. Berets also became very popular at this time, not only for general wear, but in many girls' schools the beret supplanted the old-fashioned velour crowned hat that had been part of the standard winter uniform. The navy beret also replaced the well-known Girl Guide hat. A very useful item that had been in the past: the good Guide could use it in an emergency to carry precious things to safety – the not so good Guide would place it upside down in her bicycle basket and put her newspaper-wrapped sixpennyworth of chips in it, having remembered not to have vinegar put on them as that might leak through on to her hat.

Swiftly passing on from the naughty to the nice, the 1950s woman was offered a wide selection of adornments in the way of reasonably priced jewellery to complement her outfits. At some stage most girls were given a pearl necklace. This might be fashioned from the expensive real pearls or the less expensive cultured ones, or from those which were totally artificial. A pearl necklace was often given as a 21st birthday present or a bride received one as a gift from her husband to wear on their wedding day. If this was the case, it is to be hoped that she was not superstitious. However, for some, pearls were now considered to be 'old-fashioned' – there was the terrible stigma of being seen wearing the 'old maid's' outfit of a cardigan and jumper twinset with a string of pearls, even though those young ladies who featured in the pages of *Country Life* magazine continued to display their precious family pearls. But then, those young debutantes were usually announcing their engagements, so they were all right.

For the general run of the female population, however, there was now a wide choice of new and exciting designs for necklaces, bracelets and earrings using rhinestones, diamanté and marcarsite, which came at an affordable price. Often it was possible to buy individual pieces over time to form a matching set. Then it became fashionable to wear large strings of coloured plastic beads known as 'poppits'. Each bead had a small projection that fitted into a matching small hole. No longer 'strung' on thread as was the conventional method with a necklace, the 'poppits' slotted one into the other and thus one could shorten or lengthen the necklace at will or alternatively turn it into a number of bracelets to be worn at once. Other composite materials were used to produce chunky beads; it was particularly popular to wear graded white ones with summer dresses. One fashion that has changed radically since the 1950s is the decline in clip-on earrings. Very few women then had their ears pierced. Amongst the older generation there was the feeling that this practice belonged only to the Romany population and therefore was 'not for them'. So there was a large choice of the clip-on variety and most women wore those. The biggest drawback was that after a time the spring clip became slack and the earring would fall off, or if you forgot to remove them when undressing, they could easily get caught when you were pulling a dress or jumper over your head and get lost. What then to do with the one remaining? If it was of sufficient size and interest, then the enterprising woman might turn it into a scarf clip or use it on the collar of a dress or coat as a brooch.

For the woman who could not afford to buy jewellery this was the period of experiment and many tried their hand at creating their own. Many were the brooches made at this time, either by painting designs on to a clear plastic backing that held a fastener or by pouring plaster of Paris into moulds of various shapes – small dogs seemed the most popular – or creating sprays of delicate flowers from twisted plastic-covered wire. Indeed, plastic was very much to the fore. It was possible to buy coloured plastic in different widths just as one did lengths of ribbon. Take a length of, say, pink or blue plastic ½in to ¾in wide, plus a quantity of metal D rings, weave the plastic in and out of the rings and eventually you had a unique bracelet. Plaiting several strands of plastic of shoelace thickness could produce a necklace – there were no limits to the creativity of the 1950s woman.

How many 1950s women had, as children, raided their mother's wardrobes for dressing up and been horrified to discover that a dead animal lurked there? It is hard now to imagine anyone placing a complete fox over her best Sunday costume and going off to church. The animal was placed over one's shoulder and fastened in place by a clip in the fox's mouth. Some of these furs were the standard ginger colour, while others, presumably the more expensive, were darker. These fashionable furs were available to those who could not afford a real fur coat. In the 1930s fur farming had taken place throughout the country using various animals, among them rabbits and foxes and coypu, the skin of which was traded under the name of nutria fur. It was the fearsome-looking coypu that escaped and managed to establish themselves in the countryside, causing great harm to our rivers. But it was in the 1950s that the farming of wild mink from America really took off and this was responsible for providing most of the fur trade of the period.

The 1950s woman who had been repelled by her mother wearing a whole dead fox was now quite happy to follow the fashion to have a mink collar on her winter coat and a matching mink hat and even little mink pompoms on her high-heeled shoes. If she was wealthy enough she might own a real fur stole to wear for evenings or social occasions. She might even have a full-length fur coat bought from a specialist furrier. Less expensive ones were available in the shops but buying one of those could lead to the abusive envy of one's neighbours, as one lady reported:

When I received an unexpected legacy I bought myself a grey fur coat instead of a winter coat. The first time I walked down our street, that rather common woman who lived at number 17 was cleaning her front window, and as I passed she drawled just the one word 'raabbit!' I was mortified. But I kept on wearing it.

Frances

8

Leisure Time

If the contributors to this work are to be believed, young married couples did not go out very much in the 1950s. Mr and Mrs Average may have gone to the cinema once a week or to a dance on Saturday night but most did not have the money to spend on entertainment, so they spent their evenings at home. Most people lived close enough to their workplace to be home by six o'clock, so once they had eaten their evening meal and washed up, they had at least three hours at their leisure before bedtime. This was the era before television had taken control of most people's evening activities. It is generally recognised that it was the televising of the Coronation on 2 June 1953 that persuaded families, in particular, to undertake the expense of installing a television set. Quite apart from the high price of the set itself, there was the additional quite heavy cost of installing an aerial on the roof, plus the annual licence fee. Although it was possible to hire a set at a reasonable monthly payment or to buy it on 'the never-never', as hire-purchase agreements were known, throughout the country as a whole sets were few and far between. Those who now have a 'home cinema' in their living rooms can have no comprehension of just how small those early 1950s sets were. Often housed inside a magnificent mahogany cabinet with doors, which closed when it was not in use, was a tiny screen, just 9in wide, smaller than the modern computer notebook. This meant that viewers had to sit quite close to it in order to get a clear picture. And very lucky you were if the picture was clear. Reception depended on how close one was to the local station that was relaying the signal. In those early days, only the BBC had a licence to show television programmes and even when ITV came into operation, reception in many parts of the country remained weak – a bit like broadband today!

Many people's first viewing was of a picture seen through an ultra-thick magnifying glass that overlaid the screen. These additional aids were in great demand for the Coronation, when proud television owners invited friends and members of their extended families to join them for the occasion. Often there was only one set in a whole street – you knew where it was, of course, by the aerial on the roof – and you jostled for an invitation. It seems incredible now that the daily transmission time was so short; that Sunday night programmes didn't start until after the time when evening church services ended and that each evening's programme concluded before midnight with the playing of the National Anthem. As the company assembled, curtains were drawn to shut out the daylight, the overhead electric light was extinguished, and a small table lamp, placed either on or near the set, for the sake of one's eyes, gave the only illumination. Apart from special events, television viewing at this stage was for the affluent, the elderly or families; young couples preferred to occupy their time listening to the radio, which provided plenty of diverse entertainment from variety shows, comedy programmes or plays, both original new drama or the dramatisation in serial form of classic books like *The Forsyte Saga* – which later became one of the first major Sunday night television dramas. There was plenty of opportunity too to listen to music on the radio, both on the Light Programme and on the commercial station, Radio Luxembourg, which introduced us to advertising from an early age by inducing children to become Ovalteenies. There were so many favourite radio programmes from the 1950s that, as with the novels, theatre plays and films, they will be included in appendices at the end of this book.

A young couple might not be able to afford a television set but many would save up to buy either a radiogram or a portable record player so that they could listen to their favourite music. The radiogram, as its name implies, incorporated both radio and gramophone into one impressive piece of living room furniture. This was a variation of what had existed in most homes in the 1940s: a wind-up gramophone in a simple cabinet which housed the speakers as well as space to store the records and, on top of which, stood the imposing 'wireless'. Imposing not only because of its size but because during those war years it had been the means of keeping the nation informed of the progress of the war. But the 1950s saw many of these old-fashioned pieces discarded. The wireless, especially one that was powered by a cumbersome accumulator that had to be taken to a shop to be 'topped up', was consigned to the rag-and-bone man who still toured the streets – if not with a horse and cart like Steptoe and Son, then in a lorry – while the old gramophone cabinet was likely to be recycled by an ardent DIY member of the family into a cocktail cabinet. Quite how many families actually drank cocktails is another 1950s mystery but the gramophone cabinet was not alone in suffering a makeover; in time the radiogram went the same way, as did many pianos, their interiors ripped out to be replaced with fitted lights which reflected against chromium tiles.

It was also a period when, in the urge to be 'modern', what can only be described as acts of vandalism took place.

In retrospect, although the 1950s saw great leaps forward in so many areas, it was also a period when, in the urge to be 'modern', what can only be described as acts of vandalism took place. This is not the place to draw attention to the wholesale clearing of ancient buildings in some towns and their replacement with monstrous grey cement-clad blocks of flats; I'm thinking more of artistic crazes such as that which led to the destruction of precious old 78rpm records. Someone discovered that if you heated these pre-vinyl records it was possible to mould them into interesting shapes which could be used as ornamental fruit bowls and the like. Thousands must have been sacrificed as this fad hit the country.

Fortunately, our young married wife was unlikely to have succumbed to such desecration in her efforts to beautify her home. She had much more practical projects in hand so while she and her husband listened in the evening to the radio or to records, she was busy making things. Most new housewives in the 1950s had grown up in the wartime atmosphere of 'make do and mend'. They had watched their mothers and grandmothers knitting and sewing and had learned to do likewise. What was not learned at home might be taught in school where, even from an early age, they had been encouraged to make the ubiquitous Christmas paper chains using strips of coloured paper stuck at the ends with flour and water paste. Using that same paste mixture, once newspaper or scrap paper was available, children would be taught how to make papier mâché bowls and dishes, which were then decorated using the little blocks of paint in their paintbox. While still children, girls were encouraged to make presents for members of the family for Christmas and birthdays; knitted kettle holders, pincushions and needle cases, covered coat hangers, embroidered hankies, all these were appreciated by the recipients as much, if not more, than any expensive gift today that has the child's name on it yet is known to have been paid for by the parent.

So our housewife was no novice when it came to making a house into a home. To start with there were curtains to be made for each room in the house, then there were cushion covers and padded seat covers for dining chairs, tablecloths and dressing table sets … the list went on. All these items were, of course, now available in the shops but making them yourself saved money. A popular pastime of the period, which was often a joint project, was rug making. There were two sorts of rug one could make. One had long been a standby of those on limited incomes and was made from remnants of material or rags. In its very basic form one could use an old sack, opened up to form the backing, and then, having cut up as many discarded old clothes and other bits of fabric as one could find into strips, these were threaded, a piece at a time, through the holes in the sacking to form a tuft on the right side of what would eventually become the rug. It was a time-consuming but totally satisfying operation, allowing one endless opportunity for creativity in the design, and the end result was not only colourful and unique, but it was also extremely warm to the feet. At a time when bedroom floors, for example, were still covered with cold, shiny lino, a rag mat either side of the bed was undoubtedly better than nothing at all.

However, if you had sufficient funds and you desired to have a hearthrug fitted to grace your living room, then you could take the option of buying a 'Readicut' rug kit. This, as its name implies, had everything one required to produce a decorative rug: a new canvas stamped with the design and sufficient wool, separated into each colour and all cut into the correct length, to complete the design. Full instructions were included as was the latchet hook that was needed to pass the wool back and forth. These rugs, which came either as semi-circular or the standard oblong, were most attractive, and gave not only a luxurious feel to the room but brought the couple a tremendous feeling of satisfaction. In the same way, if they had furnished their home with second-hand furniture, they could take pride and pleasure in renovating or embellishing it. For a few pence and with a bit of ingenuity a couple of orange boxes nailed together and covered with a pretty piece of offcut material could become a useful additional storage cupboard in the bedroom or bathroom.

The housewife who enjoyed handicrafts was well served by helpful magazines, including the popular monthly *Stitchcraft*, which in July 1950 cost 9*d*. Still suffering from post-war paper restrictions, this edition ran to a mere twenty-two pages, which included amongst its items a pattern for crocheted summer gloves and an 'adorable little cap you can make in an evening' made from a piece of white felt with an intricate design worked in black thread. Unfortunately, the transfer for the design as well as the pattern for the four pieces which made up the cap had to be obtained from the magazine at a cost of 8½*d* (post free). However, the enterprising housewife might be able to fabricate her own patterns. Among the patterns for jumpers, there was also an embroidered table place setting, described as a luncheon set, and a page of recipes of summer sweets – apple crumble, coffee cream and a fruit roll. Twelve months later, the magazine had risen in price to 1*s* and had thirty pages. Strangely, this issue seemed to dwell on economy, from the opening item headed 'Gay scraps make pretty motifs', which showed one how to make curtains from a piece of plain rayon with a hem in a contrasting colour above which were appliquéd flowers. The same flower transfer could be used to make a pretty apron, for, of course, the 1950s housewife always wore an apron to protect her clothes when she was cooking or serving a meal. Continuing the theme of saving, there was also a pattern for a lacy jumper and matching cardigan in two-ply wool, which was described as 'the season's smartest jumper in fine wool that saves pennies'.

As in the previous year there were also instructions for making a hat. This one was crocheted and featured an upturned brim as opposed to the close-fitting Juliet cap. There really was no excuse for the young wife not to be well turned out with all these fashionable jumper patterns available to her, and her husband was not neglected either. If she was really clever she could, in May 1952, have embarked on a bold project, a white cardigan with touches of Fair Isle patterning for herself, and for her man the matching design all over his 'attractive country pullover' – Brits had yet to adopt the word 'sweater'. This 'his and hers' ensemble was photographed in striking colour and took pride of place on the front cover, the models posed beneath a spray of pink blossom, leaning against a white picket fence, a picture of idyllic happiness. As the decade progressed fashions changed as new types of wool hit the market, and towards the end of the 1950s patterns were appearing for thick double-knit jumpers and jackets.

When our housewife tired of using her sewing machine to make dresses or run up curtains for the whole house, or plying her knitting needles to make winter hats and scarves or socks for her husband, and when she'd run out of places to put crocheted doilies and place mats, if she was enterprising she could take up her tapestry needle instead and create a picture in wool to cover a chair seat or put into a fire screen to cover the empty grate in summer. *Stitchcraft*, like the women's magazines of the period, also prepared the young housewife for eventual motherhood, and so the wise young woman carefully stored away her back issues for future use.

However, we are not to suppose that our housewife spent every evening occupied with handicrafts. If she was still holding down a job, then she would devote at least one evening to catching up on the ironing. Even if she sent her sheets to the laundry, there were still her husband's shirts to be carefully pressed. Although in those days one didn't necessarily wear clean clothes every day, your husband's work might demand a clean white shirt daily and before the arrival of easy-care cotton, that meant a lot of ironing – and without the assistance of a steam iron. No wonder then that our housewife jumped at the chance to get outside and share the gardening with her husband, both of them gaining satisfaction from growing as many of their own vegetables as possible. If they were country dwellers, or had a suburban garden that was big enough, they could well have kept hens, giving them an egg supply and the occasional treat of a roast chicken when the hen had passed its laying days.

It would seem that the average 1950s couple did not go out to eat very often. This was partly due to the fact that doing so would have been seen as an unnecessary expense and partly because opportunities were still limited. Many cafés and restaurants outside London kept shop hours and closed in the evening. Those that were open would have been considered beyond the price range of most people. It would be well into the 1960s before ordinary folk would consider entering the big hotel in the centre of town and sitting down to dine in the evening amongst those who were staying there. However, as a special treat they might have lunch in a café on a Saturday, or possibly an afternoon tea of scones and cake. If they were celebrating they might even manage a last order of sausage, beans and chips before going off to queue for the cinema on a Friday evening. If they hadn't managed to eat before the film started, then, if they were out in time, which might mean missing the last few minutes, they might catch the fish-and-chip shop before it too closed. Then, armed with their newspaper-wrapped cod and chips, they would saunter home, eating the contents prised out through the hole they had made in the wrapper with their fingers. Delicious!

The traditional English public house was still very much part of the 1950s landscape. In many ways it was still considered 'man's territory', though concessions had been made in those establishments big enough to have separate bars to have one labelled as the 'lounge bar'. Here a couple could sit on comfortable chairs at a small table rather than standing at the bar amid all the masculine talk. The 1950s wife would probably drink a Babycham, or a Britvic fruit juice, possibly a glass of Merrydown cider or, if she was very daring, a lemonade and beer shandy. It was likely too that both she and her husband smoked a cigarette while they were there and possible that they shared a packet of Smith's crisps. These were the forerunner of modern-day crisps, and were memorable because not only were they just simple plain potato but each packet contained a tiny screw of blue paper in which was the salt for you to sprinkle into the bag. The mind boggles now at the thought that in those bygone days there were workers whose job it was to place the required amount of salt on to that small square of paper and then to screw it up tight.

Years later Smith's attempted to bring back the salt, packing it into machine-sealed sachets, but it was not the same as the original.

Although a man might take his wife into the pub, women visiting on their own were not encouraged. No doubt this unspoken embargo had its roots in the ladies of the night who once used the pubs to ply their trade.

I suppose it was 1957 or 8 when my mother, aunt and I went on a week's coach tour to Scotland. I don't remember where we were staying but one evening, after dinner, accompanied by two other ladies, we went for a walk round the lovely little village set on the side of a hill. Someone suggested a drink in the local pub. I can hear it now – the deafening silence – as the five of us entered. The place was packed with men, every one of whom had turned to stare at the doorway. Not a word was said as we looked round for somewhere to sit, eventually we found a bench placed against the wall. Brazen hussy of twenty-something that I was and having lived in London, I made my way to the bar and ordered five malt whiskies! Still nothing was said, but eventually accepting the fact that we were examples of the mad English, the men continued as if we weren't there. And that might have been that but very shortly after, the landlord rushed out from behind the bar, disappeared through a doorway only to re-emerge with blankets and cloths of all shapes and sizes. It turned out a stream further up the hillside had burst its banks and it was now flowing straight towards the pub. We joined the chain for mopping-up operations and by the end of the evening, I like to think that women, whatever their nationality would thereafter have been made welcome.

Maggie

It is doubtful what impact this episode made in the general scheme of things, but many pubs had already accepted older ladies, providing them with a small portioned-off area known as 'the snug'. Anyone who has seen early episodes of *Coronation Street* will recall that 'the snug' in The Rover's Return was considered the domain of Ena Sharples and her two friends. Here they sat in the evening to set the world to rights and drink a glass of milk stout.

The pub also gave the opportunity for games such as shove-ha'penny, dominoes, darts and perhaps skittles in the adjoining skittle alley. There was no restriction on women playing either of the last two. Many women were excellent darts players but they had to be careful not to win too often. The same has to be said for card games. Many young couples would entertain themselves in the evenings with a game of cards. Again, most of them had been brought up in the previous decade when whist was very popular, both in the home and as a social function as children; they would have been taught to play whist, as well as other suitable card games. Cards crossed not only the social divide but the generations too when extended family gatherings were held. Those aspiring to ascend the social ladder learned to play bridge and could then entertain like-minded couples to an evening devoted to the game. A couple on their own might pit their wits against each other with a game of cribbage, while for an evening of bluff and double bluff and keeping a poker face there was nothing to beat a game of canasta. This was also a good game to play with friends who had come to supper or perhaps just a drink.

Pleasures were simple in those days. If our 1950s housewife was the outgoing artistic type with a good voice, she might join a choir, perhaps one belonging to her church, or the amateur operatic society or a group dedicated to performing the works of Gilbert and Sullivan. If not a singer but a musician, then it was obvious she would join with others to make music, whether it was playing chamber music or in a brass band. It was possible that our couple may have met through their mutual interest in one of these various activities, in which case they would go off to rehearsals together. Belonging to an amateur dramatics group was also very popular throughout the 1950s, giving those who took part the opportunity to enjoy acting or help backstage with scenery-making or costume design. These groups also served a much wider social purpose by presenting audiences with the opportunity to see plays that might otherwise never be within their reach. Whatever the activity in which the couple were involved, it gave purpose to their leisure time and brought them into contact with a wide circle of acquaintances.

For the couple who were not so extrovert and who were quite happy to stay in, particularly on cold winter evenings, then reading was the answer. The 1950s produced some very fine literature, most of which was available to the general public at little or no cost at all. Most urban areas had not only a central public library, which seemed to house every book ever published, but a well-stocked reference library where it was possible to go and sit in silence to study those books which you could not actually borrow. Finally, and usually near the main entrance, was a reading room that housed large, sloping easel-type structures on which were displayed most of the daily newspapers. Here you could browse your way through the important political events of the day without the expense of buying a national newspaper or, if you were job hunting, then you could scour the Situations Vacant column of the local paper. The reading room was always well used. It was warm there in winter, often providing a haven for 'gentlemen of the road' who had nowhere else to go in bad weather. Retired gentlemen often passed the time there reading while they waited for their wives to finish the shopping. In large towns the local authorities also provided smaller branch libraries in areas of dense housing, so no one was ever far from the opportunity to borrow books for free.

There were two alternatives to the free public library: the local newsagent and Boots the Chemist. Neighbourhood newsagents often had space within their shop or possibly in a back room to house several shelves of books. Presumably there was a firm that rented out mainly novels to the newsagent, rather like the videos and DVDs of more recent time. As a customer of the newsagent who delivered your daily paper, you paid a small subscription to join his library, paying threepence or so to borrow a book for a set period of time. Like the public library, a minimal fine was imposed if the book was returned late. The novels available – romances, detective stories and thrillers – catered for popular tastes. A slightly upmarket version of the newsagent–library was provided by Boots. As early as 1898, the beneficent founder of the company had put into his first shop a 'booklover's library', thus spreading his desire to offer education to all. By the 1950s a certain social cachet had developed in holding a Boots library card and it continued to offer a wide selection of both fiction and non-fiction.

Those who loved books began to build their own libraries. These were not the matching leather-bound books that were placed on a bookshelf or in a glass-fronted cabinet to impress visitors, but the books they really wanted to read. These were now brought within their scope by the paperbacks produced by Penguin, who published not just novels but a whole range of literature from classical Greek authors in translation, right through to the poetry, plays and non-fiction of the twentieth century. Penguin and Dent's Everyman series between them opened the eyes of many to the great world that lies within a book.

In considering the leisure activities of the 1950s housewife, we must not forget sports. Many young women continued to play competitive tennis, netball and hockey while they could. Their husbands probably played football, rugby and cricket, in which case the wife was likely to be involved on the domestic side by providing refreshments, particularly for cricket teas. She would also find herself washing his games kit! A wife may have accompanied her man to watch the local professional football team and both may have been keen members of their local swimming club. Membership of a golf club was often an aspiration for many rising young businessmen, but it was an expensive sport in England, though not in Scotland. Younger women were not drawn so much to golf, possibly because many clubs were still very much a male preserve, but they might well have the strong arm and good eye necessary for membership of an archery club, which provided them with exercise in the open air. All in all there was plenty to keep the 1950s housewife and her husband busy and amused.

Finally we come to what was the one leisure activity which cut across all classes of society and was probably in its heyday in the 1950s – going to the cinema. Whether one lived in a town with three or four cinemas or in a rural area, which meant a journey by bus or a bike ride to the nearest town, most people visited the cinema fairly regularly. Admission was still quite reasonably priced; if you didn't mind getting a crick in the back of your neck the first few rows closest to the screen cost as little as 1s. The back row downstairs in some cinemas had double seats, and these were usually occupied by courting couples. However, our 1950s housewife and her husband no longer needed these so they might, if they were feeling 'flush', that is, they had found an extra shilling or two in a coat pocket, venture upstairs to the more expensive seats in the circle. In those days the cinemas tended to open just after lunch, between one and two o'clock and although they gave the times that the films would be shown, the programmes ran continuously. It did not matter if you did not arrive in time for the start of the film, you took your seat anyway and waited until such time as the part you had missed came round again. Apart from the big American musicals such as *Annie Get Your Gun*, *Guys and Dolls* and *The Pajama Game*, most cinemas were still showing two films in each programme. With every 'big' picture there would be the 'B' film, perhaps a short black-and-white murder mystery with detectives in trilby hats and raincoats chasing villains in out-of-date cars that had a bell clanging on top. These films often had the audiences convulsed with laughter, although this was not the case when they were confronted with the realism of the police drama *The Blue Lamp*.

The films of the 1950s varied widely in their subject matter from those that retold the events of the Second World War, like *The Dambusters*, *The Colditz Story* and *Ice Cold in Alex*, to political comment in *I'm All Right Jack* and *Passport to Pimlico*, to sheer escapism in *High Society* and *Around the World in Eighty Days*. All these films would have been watched with pleasure and enjoyment despite the fact that many of the audience would have viewed them through a haze of cigarette smoke. In those days an ashtray was placed between every other seat, fixed to the back of the seat in front. By the end of an evening most of these were overflowing. Films were projected from a box at the rear of the cinema and occasionally it was possible to see the hovering smoke caught up in its beam. The picture being shown came on several heavy reels of film and the projectionist had to ensure that he played each reel in the correct order, making sure that the next one was wound ready to go before the previous one ran out. Occasionally mishaps occurred; the wrong reel was put on or, worse, the machine broke down causing a hiatus. It seemed then as if this always happened at the most exciting part of the film. Nevertheless, having seen a tantalising trailer for the following week's programme, most people departed for home satisfied with a good evening's entertainment.

> *All in all there was plenty to keep the 1950s housewife and her husband busy and amused.*

9

Which Twin Had the Toni?

In many ways the 1950s can be summed up by the word 'neat'. Most people strove to look neat and tidy in their person and this trait was echoed in the way they kept their homes and gardens. When one looks at photographs of the period, this desire for neatness is personified in the hairstyles.

Hairdressing in the 1950s was not the big business it is today. Certainly, outside London most hairdressers were small, often family-run businesses that bore plain, straightforward names like 'Dorothy's', 'Beryl's' or 'Jeanne's', denoting who it was who would be looking after your hair. Often the hairdresser was alone in her small shop apart perhaps for a junior apprentice. The shop was simply equipped with a washbasin, a chair, a hood hairdryer and the cumbersome piece of machinery required for permanent waving. Larger establishments often had separate cubicles divided by curtains, rather like a hospital ward, so that clients didn't watch what was being done to each other. A small counter served as a reception desk and possibly housed a telephone, as well as the appointments book. There would also be a chair for the client who arrived early for her appointment, and around the walls there would be black-and-white photographs of the latest hairstyles. The Dorothys, Beryls and Jeannes would also ensure that there was a good supply of back numbers of magazines, such as *The Lady*, *Good Housekeeping* and *Woman's Weekly*.

It was as late as 1959 that 'The Beauty Expert' of one of those magazines answered the following question from a reader called Audrey:

> How do some women manage to keep their hair so smooth and groomed looking without constantly visiting the hairdresser? I just don't seem to have much of a knack with mine.

The reply of 'The Beauty Expert' reflects the thinking of the period:

> I think some of us must face the fact that we are not gifted at hairdressing, and if one hasn't the knack, it is worth visiting a hairdresser as often as possible. Some have special arrangements for regular sets for an all-in price. If weekly visits are quite out of the question, you must practise and practise shampooing and setting until you do improve … Study a diagram to see how pin curls should be placed for a simple style (I have one I can send you if you wish). Wind your curls carefully from the scalp to the end of the hair strand and pin firmly using two grips or clips. When your hair is quite dry remove the pins and brush through it in the direction of the set. Then you can use a comb to smooth it into place … Have your hair trimmed regularly so that the length does not get out of hand, and do not wait longer than you need between perms – ask a friend to give you a home perm if necessary.

The Beauty Expert recognised the fact that very few young women, housewives in particular, could afford weekly visits to the hairdresser. Most had a regular cut every six weeks or so; some had the occasional shampoo and set, usually for a special occasion. Instead of making Audrey despondent about her hair, she offers her sensible and practical advice on hair management. The major hairdressing event, and the most expensive, was the permanent wave. This took place probably twice a year. At that period some hairdressers were using a method which involved wrapping strands of hair in silver paper and attaching them to a clip on the end of a wire that connected up to a circular overhead machine which applied heat to the hair. After what seemed like an eternity, the client would emerge with a head of waves and curls. When she returned several weeks later for a shampoo and set, her perm might be refreshed, often using old-fashioned curling tongs heated on a gas ring. Remember, electric power points were still not widely used and the hairdresser needed what she had for the hood hairdryer.

In between visits to the professionals, most women styled their own hair. Another advertising catch phrase, 'Friday night was Amami night', meant that this was when one washed one's hair. Those now accustomed to daily hair washing under the shower may find it difficult to understand exactly what was involved then. The girl who told an unwanted suitor that she was staying in to wash her hair was not exaggerating; this really was a big operation. To start with it was necessary to heat sufficient water. For those without bathrooms or a water heater above the kitchen sink, this involved filling the largest saucepan one had with cold water, placing it on the oven hotplate or gas ring, and waiting for it to come to the boil. Until that happened it was essential to make sure that the sink was clean; first removing the sink tidy with its debris of tea leaves, then giving the sink itself a scouring with Vim. That done, an appropriate jug, preferably enamel, would be placed on the draining board along with Amami shampoo. This might be in a bottle but at one time came in sachets with the measured amount ready for use. The problem with these sachets was making sure that when you snipped the corner you neither made the incision too small, thus making removal of the contents too slow, nor so deep that when you put it down before use it oozed out all over the draining board. Stripped down to your bra and/or vest, and with a towel round your shoulders, you were ready to begin. To half a jug full of hot water from the saucepan was added cold water from the tap and this was then used to wet the hair thoroughly. Next came the application of the shampoo, followed by endless rinsing in cooler water to remove all the lather. It was much easier if you had someone to help with the rinsing. If you happened to have read a beauty tip on how to achieve really shiny hair, you might splash out on a bottle of beer or raid the larder and add vinegar to the final rinse. It was believed that those people who lived in the country were fortunate in being able to use soft water drawn from a well, or rainwater from a water butt, which were considered to be much kinder to the hair.

If all this seems not only antiquated but unbelievable, we have to remember that until the introduction of immersion heaters into homes or boilers that provided constant hot water on tap, most homes had only cold water piped in from the mains, which is why most washing machines, even today, are 'cold fill'. Most bathrooms of the 1950s had a geyser over the bath that heated cold water and then filled the bath via a small pipe. Does anyone remember washbasins that had a porcelain cover where the hot tap should have been? It was only when hot taps were in place that one could then attach a rubberised hose to both taps to form a spray for hair washing. In time these were lengthened to form hand showers for the bath. The biggest drawback for both of these was that you had to make sure your tap was the right sort to take the hose and then you had to be extra careful in controlling the water pressure. Too much and one of the hoses was liable to fly off, leaving you with either freezing or almost scalding water. Alternatively, the little plastic pipe which joined the two arm pieces could disconnect itself and all the water would then run down into the sink. In many ways, the saucepan and jug method was perhaps safer.

The girl who told an unwanted suitor that she was staying in to wash her hair was not exaggerating; this really was a big operation.

After the washing came the drying. This was a long and laborious business, which may be why most women, once they had left school days and pigtails behind, opted for short hair. Personal hairdryers were not generally available so it was down either to intense rubbing with a towel or sitting on the hearthrug in front of the fire – a practice that your mother warned you would make your hair dry and brittle, quite apart from being potentially dangerous, particularly if you were using an unprotected electric fire. Once your hair was dry, and with half the evening gone, it was then time to style it. This was when you applied your second Amami product, the setting lotion. You then had the choice of using metal curlers, fortunately soon to be replaced by plastic rollers, or making pin curls, which were held in place by hairgrips. If you were recently married you would then cover your head in a rather fetching snood, a prettily coloured silk net, rather than the ordinary hairnet worn by older ladies. It was also possible to wear a turban to cover the curlers while in bed. After all that, you would rise on Saturday morning to brush out your curls. If, however, you were going somewhere special in the evening, then the curlers might remain in place all day, covered by a turban or scarf.

Then came the product that was to transform women's lives – the home perm. Like so much else at the time this came from the United States, which also gave us the catch phrase 'Which twin has the Toni?' Using identical twins the advertisement showed the attractive twins with identical hairstyles, one of whom has had a professional salon permanent wave while the other was supposed to have had a home treatment at a fraction of the cost of that of her sister. The appeal to economy was strong, as was the idea that you could achieve a professional result at home. It is said that practically every woman in the country had a home perm at some point during the 1950s. It was not an undertaking you could comfortably achieve by yourself; you needed the assistance of sister, mother, daughter or best friend to take on the task of applying the strong-smelling lotion, wrapping the papers round small clumps of hair, rolling them up on to small, pink, plastic rollers that were shaped like miniature synthetic bones for the dog, and then fixing them with a thick rubber-band-like clip. All the recipient guinea pig had to do was to sit with a little booklet of tissues, tearing out each one to hand to the operator, and sometimes to pass the rubber bands if they had become detached from the plastic roller. It was a tedious business for all concerned. It was also a practice that required accurate timing – too little and you ended up with limp curls, too much and you were stuck for weeks with frizzy hair.

The reader will have become aware of how much of life in the 1950s was influenced by advertising. Nowadays we blame television for constantly blasting us with products of every sort imaginable, but for those who don't want to see it they can simply turn off their set. In the 1950s it was difficult indeed to escape from it. To start with practically every street radiating from the centre of towns had huge billboards on which would be displayed gigantic posters advertising everything from washing powders, to drinks and cigarettes – lots and lots of those – as well as chocolates, beverages, biscuits, toothpaste, shampoos and Toni home perms. In retrospect, one can see how much that generation was brainwashed, but those hoardings served another purpose, often hiding derelict sites awaiting development. Apart from not being able to get away from the street advertising, the cinema-goer was also treated to quite a lengthy display too, though one could perhaps ignore some of these by going out to the lavatory. But then every magazine and newspaper also carried advertisements that became more eye-catching with the development of colour printing.

As the 1950s progressed hair fashions changed, influenced greatly by film stars. Younger women wanted to look like Audrey Hepburn and Leslie Caron and Doris Day, who had short, soft, curly styles. Others preferred Diana Dors' shoulder-length sleek look, with the ends gently curled under. Then, towards the end of the decade, came the beehive style. You really did need the professional hairdresser to achieve this. First came the perm and then the weekly shampoo and set, after which the bouffant effect would be achieved by vigorous backcombing, and finally would come the anchoring in place with another new development, spray lacquer. An informant related that an application of sugar water was a good substitute for the expensive spray; it certainly worked as a stiffener for petticoats but one suspects it might have made the hair attractive to wasps in summertime!

The opening of several large salons in major cities in the mid-1950s by the man nicknamed Mr Teasy-Weasy was to set the trend for the hairdressing of the future; another trendsetter was his erstwhile apprentice, Vidal Sassoon, who revolutionised the styles of the 1960s with his emphasis on good cutting. Although Raymond 'Teasy-Weasy' showed off his hair designs on television for all to see, the Dorothys, Beryls and Jeannes did not go out of business, even if in the next decade they would change their name to 'Snips' or 'Hair Magic' in an attempt to modernise. They were not trendsetters but neither were most of their clients; in fact, there were some ladies who would have been horrified to find a man doing their hair, just as several decades later there were ladies who were distressed to find that men were actually having their hair cut in Dorothy's, Beryl's or Jeanne's. This was somewhat ironic as many of these ladies quite happily sat in the gents' hairdressers and barber's shop while their young sons had their regulation school short back and sides.

Hair dyes had been available long before the 1950s, based mainly on hydrogen peroxide and henna. Those who chose to use either at home often did so with disastrous results. Achieving an overall colour was difficult and many ended up with a much richer or deeper shade than they had intended, particularly at the back of the head where one had rubbed in too much. Or it could be streaky or, worse still, the wrong proportions of chemicals could result in shades of green or purple, which at that period were neither accepted nor ignored by the public in general. So the colour shampoos which, if they went wrong, could be rectified by constant washing, were welcome indeed. Nevertheless, the housewife who could afford it might consider a professional colour treatment, but she had to bear in mind that once she had started on that path, she would have to continue.

Hair dyes had been available long before the 1950s, based mainly on hydrogen peroxide and henna. Those who chose to use either at home often did so with disastrous results.

It would be these more affluent ladies who would also make use of the other beauty services available in the hairdressing salon such as eyebrow shaping or manicures. But there was another type of hair which was receiving more attention in the 1950s and that was what was delicately referred to as superfluous hair; that is, the downy moustache that was the bane of many women's existence. Since time immemorial this has been a problem for women, especially brunettes. Many remedies have been tried throughout the ages, one of the most unusual from the eighteenth century being the application to the area of a mixture of pigeon dung and urine. Hydrogen peroxide was the more modern method. The problem with that was that skin was whitened too, so that the hair was still noticeable. Other methods in use in the twentieth century included pumice-like stones or mitts that were rubbed over the offending hair. Done too roughly and the woman rubbed off her skin, resulting in nasty sores. Home waxing was also available. A kit containing a small metal container with a fold-down handle held a lump of wax which was then heated on the gas ring or electric hob. Once melted, the softened wax was applied to the upper lip and allowed to harden. Then it was time to grasp the end of the strip and remove it with a sharp tug. The treatment was successful if somewhat painful; its worst feature being the lingering smell of the heated wax.

During the 1950s discreet advertisements appeared, mainly in the broadsheets, for a clinic which offered electrolysis. This involved a thin needle-like probe attached to an electrical machine being placed into individual hair follicles. It was not particularly painful and was supposed to kill off or retard new growth but there was a limit as to how much could be achieved in a session, so a course was advised, and it was expensive. Another method using electricity known as diathermy was similar to electrolysis but, in this case, the client had to have her hand in a bowl of water to make an electrical circuit for the probe. Little wonder that the more fearful woman resorted to plucking (frowned upon by the beauty magazines), Veet (really intended for treatment on coarse leg hair) or her husband's razor.

10

In Her Shopping Basket She Has ...

Shopping today is so vastly different to what it was in the 1950s. Young people must find it hard to comprehend what life was like before the advent of huge shopping malls and out-of-town superstores which sell everything imaginable from bananas to butter, cosmetics to curtains, television sets to tea bags – feel free to add your own items! The changes in our shopping habits have been influenced by a number of things but as usual it was the American style that led the way to self-service food stores, and the increase in personal transport that fostered the growth of the out-of-town developments. Suddenly too, we all became so frantically busy that we had no time to wait for a friendly assistant to weigh out our butter, cheese or sugar. How much easier it was to grab things off the shelves, stuff them into a wire basket or trolley, even if we then had to wait in a queue to pay for them. Then, during more affluent times, it seemed more sensible not to do a weekly shop but to stock up for the whole month on certain things, much of which would go into the freezer, and pay for everything on a credit card.

It was only towards the end of the 1950s that ordinary people started buying fridges. These were bulky machines, mostly with a rounded front, that contained a small ice-making compartment that took up most of the top shelf and an interior capacity that seemed small in relation to the overall size of the machine. Those with spacious kitchens had room for the much larger, usually

American-made, machines, which had such refinements as an iced water dispenser. Deep freezers made their real impact in the 1960s when the larger chest ones intended for commercial use were cheaper to buy than the smaller domestic units. Canny buyers who had a garage with space to spare or a secure outhouse bought the larger models and unwittingly set the trend for the use of the garage for many years to come.

We have already established that the 1950s housewife usually shopped daily for the fresh ingredients of the main meal of the day. Unlike today's housewife she tended to visit a number of different shops and she bought in small quantities. Since most wives had a set amount of money available for housekeeping they learned to shop wisely in order to make sure that there was enough to last for the week. The prudent woman had probably adopted her mother's habit of keeping a weekly account book. In this she would list the basic items she needed: a ¼lb packet of tea (loose leaves not tea bags), ½lb of butter, the same of cheese, mainly Cheddar, and cooking fat (lard or Trex) – cooking oil was unheard of, while for most people olive oil was still something you obtained in small quantities from the chemist and used warmed to cure earache. Britons were, of course, still using imperial measures, so everything came in pounds and ounces. Eggs, flour, jam and marmalade, peanut butter, Marmite, Bovril or Betox, cocoa or Ovaltine, ½lb of bacon, back for preference, streaky if you were hard up – these were likely to feature regularly, if not weekly, on the list. It could be enlivened with occasional treats such as Libby's tinned fruit, peaches or fruit cocktail, evaporated milk and the inevitable Bird's Custard powder.

Most of these could be obtained from one of the old established grocers in one's neighbourhood. The housewife would set out with her wicker shopping basket either looped over her arm or held in her hand, depending on its size and shape. These could be quite elegant and to a newlywed made her feel very grown up and really married. The present of a really good basket (the equivalent of a designer label) for a birthday or at Christmas was greeted with great pleasure. In many towns there was a basket shop that displayed and sold baskets that were hand made in the local workshop for the blind. It was only as we became more affluent that the basket ceased to be able to hold all that had been purchased, and baskets or bags on wheels were introduced. These were later discarded in favour of carrier bags, both paper and plastic, to suit the throwaway society we were becoming. Strange isn't it that sixty years on hard economic times mixed with a social conscience has turned us back, if not to baskets, at least to shopping bags made of recyclable materials which, although utilitarian, have given designers scope to make them attractive to the user even if they are mainly used to carry goods from the supermarket to car boot.

Having placed her order, the 1950s customer could sit on the chair in front of the counter as the grocer or his assistant assembled each item in front of him, making conversation as he did so, perhaps discussing the merits of different brands of baked beans before ticking off each item in the order book and noting its price in the column down the side. This allowed the customer the chance to compare current prices with those of previous weeks and if the rise was too much she would

Ask any woman who was either a child or a housewife in the 1950s for memories of shopping and without a doubt she will mention Sainsbury's.

know where to make cuts the following week. Her basket was then packed for her, the column of figures added up, and the pounds, shillings and pence in her purse passed either across the counter or taken to the small kiosk in the corner where the matriarchal lady who dealt with matters financial reigned aloof from all. However, if our housewife shopped at her local Co-op store, the chances were that they still retained the wondrous system whereby your money, plus the ticket bearing your dividend share number, was placed into a small metal cup, then fastened to an attachment on a wire just above the assistant's head. At a pull on the small handle it was sent whizzing across the ceiling to the cashier's desk, which was slightly elevated in a glass cubicle. The larger department stores, many of which still retained the surname of their late Victorian founder, had a more sophisticated system than the overhead one used by the Co-op. Each department tended to have open counters arranged in a square with a space in the centre. The glass counters held display cabinets both under and on them. The area in the middle held storage drawers that were easily accessible to the assistants from their station behind the counter. If you find it difficult to visualise this, it may help to think of the television programme *Are You Being Served?* The background music to that programme contained the sound of the ringing of cash registers but can you remember seeing one? In a central area close to each set of counters was a large pillar that went up to the ceiling. At waist height there were small mesh baskets attached to openings in the pillar. Each basket held a metal tube 5in or 6in in length that had pads at either end. When an assistant had completed a sale and collected the cash from the customer, this was placed with the sales details into the tube, which in turn was placed in the wall opening – and hey presto – it magically disappeared with a whoosh, only to reappear in the basket within minutes, complete with a receipt and the correct change. You must forgive this rather clumsy recollection of a child who never ceased to marvel at the mystery of the hows and whys of this miracle machine.

Of course, not all shops were owned by independent traders. Every town possessed at least one branch of one of the nationwide chains such as The Maypole, The International, David Greig, Elmers, Kays, The Home and Colonial, Liptons and Sainsbury's. In time each of these developed multiple service counters where the customer moved from one to the other. Ask any woman who was either a child or a housewife in the 1950s for memories of shopping and without a doubt she will mention Sainsbury's. Their shops tended to be long and narrow from front to back with one long counter stretching down each side. Gleaming white-patterned tiles covered the walls and with the chequerboard tiled floor they created an aura of ultra cleanliness. All the assistants wore white overalls and caps on their heads. But it was the butter and cheese counters that evoked most memories. With hindsight this may have been a reaction to the after-effects of rationing but who could not fail to be impressed by those enormous mounds of golden butter that stood against the walls? And how we marvelled at the mastery of the assistant who, with two large wooden paddles, could remove a small piece from the yellow mountain, pat it into a neat rectangle which, when placed on the scales, weighed exactly the 8oz that had been requested. To those who had grown up accustomed to taking their butter ration as it came it was sheer delight to be able to choose if one would have English butter or that from New Zealand or Denmark, salted or unsalted. Choice was governed by price or preference for taste.

Similarly there was now a choice of cheeses. Like the butter, whole wheels of cheese were on display and again one would admire the precision with which the assistant would cut your desired amount with a very fine wire ready for the scales. These scales themselves were worth looking at. Made of brass with a pan either side of a central beam, your butter or cheese was placed in one pan and the different weights, also made of brass, some of which resembled chess pieces, were placed in the other. From dairy products one would pass down the counter to where the large, red, somewhat frightening, slicing machine held pride of place. Here were to be found whole sides of bacon and hams, and again one could choose exactly how much of which one wanted. You watched almost breathlessly as the circular blade of the slicer passed through the bacon or ham joints cutting to the thickness for which you had asked. Your order was then carefully wrapped in greaseproof paper. And so you worked your way up and down the counters. As each item was purchased the customer was given a small ticket bearing the price of the item, and before she left the shop she would take these to settle her bill at the polished wood, glass-fronted cashier's desk that was situated at the far end of the shop.

If the housewife was shopping in town and had decided she needed fish for that evening's meal, then the chances were her next stop would be at MacFisheries. Here, the whole front of the shop was open to the street so one could smell the fish as well as admire the assortment displayed on the marble slabs with lots of ice cubes and fresh, or occasionally artificial, parsley dividing the different types. The wall at the rear of the shop was often lined with panels of tiles embossed with appropriate underwater and fishy designs. The assistants wore blue-and-white-striped aprons and boaters just as they had done for generations. They were always ready to oblige their customers by gutting or filleting a fish, dressing a crab or simply providing them with pieces to make fish stock – or maybe to feed the family cat. MacFisheries did not hold the monopoly on fish sales; most towns had at least two other independent traders offering customers a choice, which might depend as much on price as personal taste.

That same choice applied to butchers. In the 1950s there were still specialist pork butchers where you could buy your pork joints, bacon, ham and sausages, as well as pork pies, pig's liver and kidneys, and black pudding. But there were also other delights, some of which were very reasonably priced, like their own home-made potted meat; pork cheese or brawn, full of meaty jelly and delicious with a salad in summer; faggots, haslet and chitterlings. Plus, as everyone knows, since there is very little of the pig that is not edible, the less squeamish might buy a pig's head, trotters and the tail. At Christmas time the pork butcher was likely to have a pig's head as the centrepiece of his window display. As in the coloured plates in old-fashioned cookery books, the head was decorated with different coloured icing and an apple was always placed in its mouth.

The ordinary butcher's shop usually still had sawdust on the floor to make it easier to clear up any blood or bits of bone and shavings of meat which might fall when joints were being cut up. Large carcases were suspended on metal hooks on the wall behind the serving counter. Below them was the scrubbed wooden saw bench and, as our housewife watched, it was on this that the butcher chopped or sawed through bones before cutting off the joint she had requested with a lethally sharp knife. Your butcher could be your best friend for he not only knew how each joint should be cooked, but could also advise the novice cook on what would be right for her budget. He would cut the stewing beef or shin for a pie or casserole into cubes and add just the right amount of ox kidney if she was making a steak and kidney pudding, usually throwing in for nothing the lump of suet she would need to make the pudding crust. Like most food retailers of the period, butchers prided themselves on their attractive year-round window displays. In the run up to Christmas he would ask our housewife if she wanted him to put a bit of silverside or brisket into his brine bath to turn into salt beef, while in the final week or so before the holiday chickens, turkeys, geese and game birds, still with their feathers on, would hang up in rows both behind the counter and sometimes, during opening hours, outside the shop itself. It was like looking at an illustration from Dickens' *A Christmas Carol* where Scrooge instructs the boy in the street to run and buy the big goose. In those early 1950s before every butcher had cold store facilities and the shop was to be closed for the two days of Christmas, those who were willing to take a gamble by not buying their bird until just before closing on Christmas Eve could find themselves the proud owner of a goose or chicken for half the price it had been the day before.

Continuing with her shopping, our housewife might next visit a bakery and confectioner's shop for a fresh crusty loaf of bread and perhaps, if mother-in-law was coming to tea on Sunday, a cake. Faced with the array of chocolate éclairs, iced buns, Eccles cakes and cream doughnuts, all freshly made on the premises, our housewife might decide to play it safe and select instead a Fuller's iced Madeira cake. This was always very popular, as were a Battenberg or a Lyons chocolate Swiss roll. The cream in that had a taste that has never been recaptured down the years; neither has that lovely thick wodge found in the centre of the roll. If the bakery was part of one of the chains, such as the ABC which stood for the Aerated Bread Company, then the shop might have had a small café in the back where one could, if one so wished, sit down and have a cup of tea before continuing with the shopping.

Our housewife did not spend all her time on food shopping. If she needed a new hat, for example, she again had choice from among the specialist milliners, of which there were usually several in town, often bearing the name of the owners, such as the expensive-sounding 'Madame Violette' or the more down to earth 'Pansy Peck'. It is possible that the very term 'millinery' has fallen into disuse, rather as the wearing of hats has. But in the 1950s there were still skilful ladies who could make a hat for you to wear for a special occasion, as well as keeping a good stock of ready-made ones, copies of which they could guarantee would not be found on the counters of Marks & Spencer or British Home Stores. Having browsed the milliners' windows, it was on to one of many wool shops. The housewife might have been there to collect the last few ounces of wool for the cardigan she was making for her husband. If she had needed quite a lot and it was quite expensive to buy all at once the proprietor would have been quite happy to 'put the skeins aside' for the customer to pay as she collected them. This putting to one side had the added advantage that all the wool came from the same batch and should therefore be the correct colour. There was nothing worse than running out of wool just before completing a garment and then finding that you were unable to match the exact shade required.

Apart from the plethora of wool shops, most towns also supported sewing-related shops. In the shops Leisure Hours, Busy Fingers and Spare Moments the enthusiast could buy linen to embroider or a design-ready printed tray cloth or tablecloth that came with the directions as to which of the wide range of Clark's Anchor stranded silks should be used to complete it. Here too were to be found not only the different types of canvas for tapestry work and the accompanying wools but also frames for holding the work in progress. One never seemed to be hurried in these establishments as like-minded ladies congregated to discuss the relative merits of different items. In retrospect, one wonders how all these small, often duplicated shops managed to make a living for as long as they did.

The answer may be twofold. First, most of them that catered specifically for women were run by women; wives whose husbands had their own jobs so that the shop was not the only source of income. Second, the shop invariably came with living accommodation both behind

One never seemed to be hurried in these establishments as like-minded ladies congregated to discuss the relative merits of different items.

and above the premises. This meant that the shopkeepers had only one set of rates, rent and utilities to pay rather than the two they would have had if they had a home elsewhere. The shift of population from living over the shop to new out-of-town estates, plus the change in shopping habits, has led to the shameful waste of good living space in towns. Changes in ownership as well as change in use of the shops led either to offices taking over the upper floors or it being used only for storage. The twenty-first-century town streets are not only full of empty shops but, worse still, beautifully proportioned Victorian and Edwardian accommodation, which once housed families who were very much part of the community, are left to crumble away.

For the 1950s housewife the aforementioned prospect is unthinkable as she makes her way past thriving shops and bustling crowds. And now that she has done all her shopping and doesn't need to hurry home because her husband will not yet have returned from either playing in a match himself or watching the local football team, she may meet a friend at one of the many tea rooms or cafés in town. There were those behind specialist coffee shops like the Kardomah where the smell of coffee roasting in a machine in the window wafted out into the street, enticing customers to come in. Then there were a number of smart, elegant tea rooms with waitresses in black dresses and frilly white aprons, with matching bands that went round their foreheads. Here the 1950s housewife could treat herself to a speciality tea – very daringly she might try one from China rather than the everyday Indian to which she was accustomed, and she would eat her chosen cake or pastry with a pastry fork, something she rarely, if ever, used at home. Alas, such elegance was not to last. Gradually the tea rooms would become either self-service snack bars or, towards the end of the decade, coffee bars. Then out went the white tablecloths, wooden chairs and delicate china to be replaced with chromium tubular chairs, red Formica-topped tables, and glass cups and saucers. Tea was out and frothy coffee, sweetened with brown sugar, quite unlike anything we'd ever had before, was in. And with it came yet another American craze, the jukebox. No longer would our 1950s housewife be able to relax over her tea and scones while a lady pianist accompanied a violinist in a selection of gentle popular classics to soothe away the cares of the day.

11

A Bicycle Made for Two ...

Daisy was not a particularly popular name for the 1950s housewife, but our woman would have been no stranger to a bicycle. Having learned to ride one as a child, the chances are that she would have had to own one once she went to senior school. In many households it was cheaper to buy a second-hand bike than contemplate the weekly cost in bus fares over the next five years. Also, once the girl started out to work, unless her employment was within walking distance, then she would take it for granted that she would cycle there.

It would be fair to say that cycling was the most common form of transport for the majority of the workforce of this country during the 1950s. Even those who lived in the capital or in one of our larger industrial cities where the streets were crowded used bicycles. There were, of course, far fewer cars on the roads then. Even when petrol rationing ceased and the motor manufacturers began to produce new cars, these were seen very much as luxury items, as indeed they were, for the purchase tax of 33 per cent, added to the retail cost, put a new car well beyond the means of the man in the street. During the war petrol rationing had restricted the use of a car to civilians whose livelihood depended upon it, such as doctors, farmers, certain tradesmen, commercial travellers and so on. Ask those who recall the 1950s how many cars there were in their street at that time and you will be surprised how few, if any, there were.

So in many ways the reliance on the bicycle for transport had become ingrained in the population. A cycle could be purchased for a moderate price, and since these sturdy, well-built machines lasted for years, required little maintenance, beyond the occasional new tyre, the weekly pumping up of those tyres and the application of a bit of oil in the right places, they were a good investment. If you bought new, you knew you could sell for a good price in the future should you need to. Machines were passed down through family members many years after the initial purchase and even then might find yet another owner.

Most of those questioned continued to ride their bicycles after marriage, as did their husbands. There are archive pictures on newsreels of manual workers leaving work at the end of their shift and the majority are on bicycles. Any new factory built at the time had to incorporate a covered area for bicycle racks; certainly only a fraction of the space required nowadays for car parking. In fact, wherever one worked, whether shop or office, there was usually enough space to store one's bike safely. Public libraries provided cycle racks for the use of borrowers while shoppers would simply place a pedal flat on the kerb and there stood your bike – though if you were going to be some time it might be a wise precaution to padlock the wheel to deter any would-be thief.

If the bike was important for the town dweller, it was a vital lifeline for those who lived in the country. With a restricted or even non-existent bus service, the country dweller without a bicycle would have had to walk everywhere. With changes in agricultural employment, walking to work was no longer an option; similarly with the mergers of village schools. Also, without their two wheels many in rural areas would have had no social life whatsoever outside their immediate locality. Countrywomen in the 1950s talk of riding with their husbands to the next village to attend a dance, wearing their best frocks and with their high heels in the front basket or in the saddlebag. I am assured that it could be quite romantic riding home through country lanes on a crisp, moon-bright winter's night.

If the bike was important for the town dweller, it was a vital lifeline for those who lived in the country.

The vehicle chosen to woo Daisy was a tandem and these became very popular with some young married couples in the 1950s, providing them with the opportunity to go out at weekends, particularly in summer, to explore the countryside around their town or city. Both bicycles and tandems would later also be able to accommodate a child. The next step up from pedal power was the motorbike. Many young men had wooed their future wives on one of these and, she having become used to riding pillion (neither of them wearing the now compulsory helmet), they continued to make use of it. In many cases, the husband rode it to and from work. The very fact of his owning the machine widened the range within which he could seek employment. In the same way, astride their motorcycle, the couple could visit locations much further away from home at the weekend. During the 1920s sidecars had been attached to these petrol-driven machines and the 1950s saw a resurgence of their use, giving the couple the choice of being able to accommodate a passenger on an outing. Once pregnant, and after the child was born, the wife could still enjoy outings from the comfort of the sidecar.

By the time the 1960s dawned, many motorbikes would have been swapped for the more modern nippy little Lambrettas and Vespers or the covered versions that became the original three-wheeled cars, the Messchermitz and the BMW Isetta. Dubbed 'bubble cars', and powered by motorbike engines, they had two wheels at the front and one at the rear. It was possible to seat three adults, two at the front and one at the rear. They, and variations of them, were fun to drive while still remaining economical. In many ways, both scooters and bubble cars sum up the mood of the period. Gone were the dark post-war days, gone too the need to be cautious, instead a new youthful generation determined to have fun was on the rise.

While 'teenagers' were creating themselves in the second half of the decade, some of those who had married throughout the 1950s were now earning enough to consider buying a car. Probably not a new one, but second hand, possibly even one that dated back to the 1930s. Most young men had learned to drive while doing their National Service and finally they were able to use the skill they had acquired. Only a handful of women drove before the war, mainly those from the upper middle classes, and these were the girls who, as members of the ATS for example, often found themselves as drivers for high-ranking officers. Others, like the then Princess Elizabeth drove – and maintained – heavy army lorries. These women, having married professional men with good salaries, would no doubt have continued to drive, possibly even having a car for their personal use. But that was not the norm. Just because her husband had bought a family car, it did not mean that his wife would be allowed to drive it. Driving was men's work! A woman could not be expected to know about such things; she certainly couldn't be trusted to take it out on the road all by herself and if she wanted to go somewhere, well he would take her, providing it was at a convenient time for him. If they were going out together, of course he would drive for what would the neighbours think if they saw him being driven by his wife?

It took a long time to break down this particular barrier, helped in part by the law on drinking and driving. As late as the mid-1970s a mother was heard telling her small daughter that they were going for a ride in Daddy's car – not, you will note, 'the car' but specifically 'Daddy's car'. That mother, like so many wives of the 1950s, was never given the opportunity to learn to drive. Sadly, there are a vast number of older women who, when they were widowed, found themselves with a perfectly good car in the garage which was useless as far as they were concerned. Others had to wait until they were in their 40s and 50s before they could take driving lessons, only to find that just after they had achieved their independence at the driving wheel, their husbands retired and wanted to do all the driving themselves!

Having established what were the most popular modes of personal transport in the 1950s, let us consider that question – most frequently heard in the hairdresser's salon – where are you going for your holiday this year? During the 1950s most workers, the majority of whom worked a five-and-a-half-day week, were entitled to two weeks of paid holiday, in addition to the bank holidays of Christmas and Boxing Day, Easter Monday, Whit Monday and August bank holiday Monday, which in those days fell on the first Monday of that month rather than on the last as nowadays. There was a strong link between personal modes of transport and holidays. It was not until the end of the decade that people were seriously considering using

TROUSSEAU.

✓ Grey Coat suit	13 . 0 .	
✓ Shoes	4	19
✓ Han bag	4	0
✓ Gloves	1	5
✓ 2 pr nylons	1	5
✓ Vests	1	1
✓ 3l Bras		16
Panties		10
✓ Nightdress	3	14
✓ Shortie Pyjamas	1 . 3 .	
✓ Housecoat	3	17
✓ Cotton dress	2	19
✓ Silk dress .	4	7
✓ Swim suit .	4	4
Swimming cap		
✓ Perm .	4	16
✓ Blouse	2	19
✓ Hat Girdle	1	9
✓ Cotton skirt	3	10

1. A bride lists her trousseau with prices.

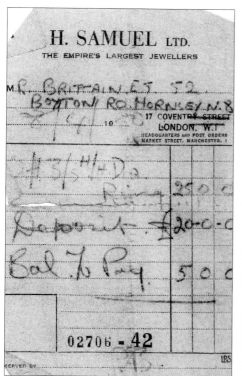

2. The bridegroom-to-be was £5 short when he bought the second-hand diamond engagement ring.

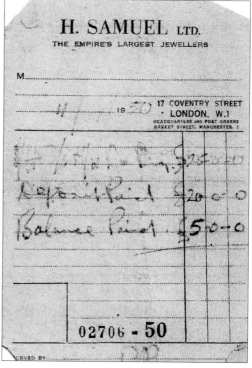

3. H. Samuel's receipt for the balance.

4. One of a set of three EPNS spoons given by Bravingtons on the purchase of a wedding ring.

5. Wedding style – 1951.

6. Wedding style – 1952. Note the interested bystanders.

7. Wedding style – 1953.

8. Wedding style – 1955. This bride caught the hem of her dress as she alighted from the hire car. The vicar's wife came to the rescue with a needle and thread.

9. Wedding style – 1957. Modern 'ballerina-style'.

10. Jean's family group.

11. Diane's family group. Note the bride's mother's fur stole.

PRESENT	FROM	ACK'D.
Cheque	Mr. & Mrs. R. W. Wheeler	4. 6. 56.
Uncle Alec & Auntie Emily	Prestige kitchen set and coffee service	17. 6. 56.
Mr. and Mrs. Offord	Phoenix glassware	25. 6. 56
Uncle Felix and Aunt Mary.	Sherry glasses and tray	25. 6. 56
Mr. and Mrs. Booth	Wine glasses	2. 7. 56
Richard Wheeler	Dinner service	15. 7. 56
Dr. and Mrs. Hyde	Wooden fruit bowl	29. 6. 56
Kathleen, Norman & Judith	Table linen	29. 6. 56
Jill and Susan	Towels	7. 7. 56
Mr. and Mrs. Scougal	Rowson Table Lighter.	7. 7. 5
Mr. and Mrs. Woodfield	Cheque	9. 7. 56
Mrs E. Armstrong	Towels	7. 7. 5
Dr. Martin	Pillow cases	15. 7. 56
Ann and Charles	Table mats	14. 4. 56
Mrs. Counter	Bath towel	14. 4. 56
Staff at school	Cheque	16. 7. 56
Mr. Gunn & Mr. Ristow	Table mats	16. 7. 56
Mr. & Mrs Kite	Tea service	15. 4. 56
H. Mummack	Bottle of sherry	13. 7. 5
Mr. & Mrs. Lauder.	Teapot	15. 7. 5
Mrs Holt. William	Kumfi-Kut scissors	16. 7. 5
Desmond Filby	Morphy-Richards steam iron	15. 7. 5
Christopher Filby	Electric kettle	15. 7. 56

12. Some of the presents one bride received. Note the date she acknowledged each gift.

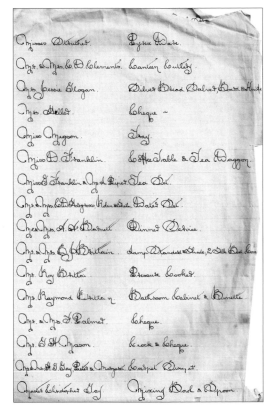

13. A bridegroom carefully recorded these gifts.

14. Prefabricated houses dating from the late 1940s – still in occupation.

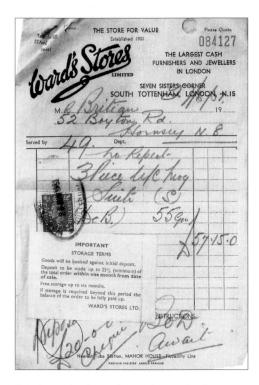

LIVING ROOM.

Small carpet
✓ Rug
✓ Fire Screen
✓ Dining Table
✓ Dining chairs
✓ Space frame unit
✓ 2 armchairs
✓ 1 settee
✓ Trolley
✓ light fitting
✓ Radiogram
✓ Canteen of cutlery
✓ water set
✓ Sherry glasses
Port glasses
✓ White wine glasses
✓ Whisky glasses
✓ Magazine rack
✓ Portable electric fire
✓ Curtains.
✓ Coal hod.
✓ Companion set.
✓ Table mats.

15. A list of requirements for a living room.

16. A receipt for a three-piece suite in uncut moquette.

✓ Cruet	BEDROOM.
✓ Wooden fruit bowl	✓ Bed
Bread Board and Knife	✓ 4 Pillows
✓ Fish knives and forks	✓ Rug or carpet
✓ Tray	✓ Wardrobe
	✓ Eiderdown
	✓ Curtains
	✓ Light fitting
	✓ 8 Pillowcases (top)
	✓ 12 Pillowcases (under)
	✓ 2 Blankets
	✓ 1 Lam. Air. Cel Blanket.
	✓ 1 under blanket
	✓ 6 Hand towels
	✓ 2 Bath sheets
	✓ 2 Guest towels
	✓ 3 prs double sheets.

17. Requirements for the bedroom.

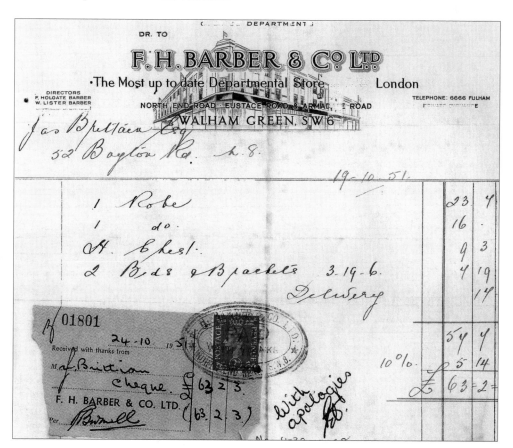

18. Receipt for bedroom furniture.

HALL
- Rug
- Light fitting
- Doormat.
- Table

BATHROOM
- Medicine cupboard
- Bathmat
- Sponge and soap rack.
- Linen box stool.
- Light fitting

KITCHEN.
- Cooker
- Table
- 2 Stools
- Matting
- 3 Saucepans
- Frying pan
- Steamer
- Electric kettle
- Percolator
- Yorkshire Pudding tins
- Roaster
- 3 Cake tins
- Colander
- Washing up bowl
- Bucket.
- 2 Phoenix casseroles
- 3 Phoenix plates (various)
- Prestige 1900 kitchen set
- Sky-line chef set.
- Prestige egg whisk
- Prestige general purpose knife
  Plate rack
- Storage tins (coffee, tea, sugar etc)

19. Requirements for kitchen and bathroom.

20. Modern designs for china by Midwinter.

21. A 1950s housewife in her modern kitchen. *Courtesy of Hearst Magazines*

22. Another view of her kitchen. *Courtesy of Hearst Magazines*

23. A 1950s refrigerator. *Courtesy of Hearst Magazines*

Progress in the Home

Hoover Limited take pride in the fact that their products are saving millions of housewives from hard, wearisome drudgery — not only in Britain but throughout the world. Wherever the name Hoover appears it is a guarantee of excellence.

THE WORLD-FAMOUS HOOVER CLEANER

The Hoover Cleaner, with its famous triple-action principle — " It beats . . . as it sweeps . . . as it cleans " — is undeniably the world's best cleaner — best in design, best in materials, best in quality of workmanship. There is a model suitable for every size and type of home.

THE MARVELLOUS HOOVER ELECTRIC WASHING MACHINE

The Hoover Electric Washing Machine has completely revolutionised the whole conception of washing-day in the home. It does the full weekly wash for a large family and yet is such a handy size—suitable for even the smallest kitchen.

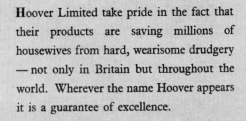

VISIT THE HOOVER FACTORY

Visitors to the Festival of Britain are cordially invited to make a tour of the Hoover Factories at Perivale, Middlesex, or Merthyr Tydfil, South Wales, or Cambuslang, Scotland. Please write to, Hoover Limited, Perivale, or 'phone Perivale 3311 for more information.

HOOVER LIMITED

Factories at :

PERIVALE, MIDDLESEX · MERTHYR TYDFIL · HIGH WYCOMBE · CAMBUSLANG, SCOTLAND

24. Advertisement for Hoover appliances that appeared in the 1951 Festival of Britain Guide. *Courtesy of Hoover-Candy*

THE TIME TO LOOK AHEAD

GOOD LOOKS AND COMFORT COMBINE IN THESE THREE DESIGNS

DON'T you like a dress which can be made to look "different"? Bestway Dress Pattern No. D 3431 is cut on well-tried lines but has an unusual collar through which a gay scarf can be slotted to ring the changes.

USE a delicate floral print for the soft lines of Bestway Dress Pattern No. E 2502. There are many fabrics to choose from and they emphasize perfectly the femininity of the gathered bodice and gently billowing skirt.

HERE is a dress that is simple to slip into, and as fresh as a spring breeze. The bodice of Bestway Dress Pattern No. D 3876 is spiced with a neat strap which continues into the skirt and is fitted with sprung darts.

BESTWAY PATTERN No. D 3431
Price 2/9
(Including postage and packing.) Cut in bust/hip sizes 36/40, 38/42, 40/44, 42/46, 44/48 and 48/52 inches.

BESTWAY PATTERN No. E 2502
Price 2/7
(Including postage and packing.) Cut in bust/hip sizes 32/36, 34/38, 36/40, 38/42 and 40/44 inches.

BESTWAY PATTERN No. D 3876
Price 2/9
(Including postage and packing.) Cut in bust/hip sizes 32/36, 34/38, 36/40, 38/42 and 40/44 inches.

D 3876. In 36-inch material allow 4¼ to 4½ yards or 4 to 4½ yards with short sleeves.

These Paper Patterns are obtainable only by post and NOT from any shop or store. Orders should be addressed to WOMAN'S WEEKLY Paper Pattern Department, P.O. Box 653, 21, Whitefriars Street, London, E.C.4.
Write, giving the Pattern Number, and please don't forget to state the bust size required. Money should be sent by Postal Order made payable to The Amalgamated Press, Ltd., and crossed " & Co." Overseas readers can obtain delivery of these patterns by mail from our London Pattern Dept. at the stated prices.

(centre) E 2502. Allow 4 to 4½ yards of 36-inch width or 4½ to 4⅜ yards with ¾-sleeves.

(left) D 3431. Allow 4¼ to 5¼ yards of 36-inch width material.

25. Dress patterns in 1959. *Courtesy of* Woman's Weekly

EASTERN ELECTRICITY BOARD
NORTHMET SUB-AREA
ELECTRICITY OFFICES & SHOWROOM, THE BROADWAY, CROUCH END, N.8.
Telephone: MOUntview 8282

Cash Sale
& J Brittain Esq
143 Crouch Hill
N 8.

Regd. No.

Invoice No. **6621**

30 - 5 - 195...

	Quantity	Pattern No.	Description	Rate	£	s.	d.
	1		English Electric 2009 Cooker (reconditioned) Serial No:- 10504		£19	10	0

All accounts are net and payable within 21 days of delivery.

Cheques, etc. should be made payable to the "Eastern Electricity Board" and crossed "A/c payee."

For future requirements of

APPLIANCES

EASTERN ELECTRICITY BOARD

Received at NORTHMET. SUB-AREA District Office	Account No.	Amount Received £ s. D
		-1 9- 10 · 0

26. Receipt for a 1950s reconditioned electric cooker.

27. 1957 hairstyles and summer clothes.

28. Sixth form girls visiting Stratford-upon-Avon in 1958. Note that their school uniform dresses show signs of having the fashionable starched petticoats beneath.

29. A group of happy campers at Corton Beach Holiday Camp in 1950.

"I BLESS THE DAY I WROTE FOR IT"

It's odd how one simple action can brin[g] such long-lasting benefits! Many an[d] many a woman, hearing some moder[n] minded friend praising Tampax, ha[s] sent for a sample, and found an amazin[g] difference in her life. Undreamed [of] comfort. Simplicity in use. Suc[h] tremendous advantages over ol[d] fashioned methods. And such *securit[y]*

A Confidential Trial

If you are modern-minded enough t[o] test the extra daintiness, comfort an[d] peace of mind that Tampax brings, d[o] so *in confidence*. Just send sixpence i[n] stamps to The Nurse, Dept. 17[,] Tampax Ltd., Belvue Road, Northol[t] Middlesex, for a trial packet in plai[n] cover, with fully informative literatur[e] You too may bless the day!

TAMPAX

Sanitary Protection Worn Internal[ly]

TAMPAX LIMITED, BELVUE ROAD, NORTHOLT, MID[

this year . . .

next year . . .

sometime . . .

never . . .

NOW . . .

No one has yet found a better way of knowing when you're going to fall in love! But there are better ways of deciding other things . . . such as when to start a family.

The arrival of children is something that need not be left to chance . . . and *must* not be, if you want your future family to be a deeply happy one.

Full information on Family Planning is not difficult to obtain.

For your own sake, and your family's, find out about it—not this year . . . not this week . . . but *now*.

PLANNED FAMILIES
PUBLICATIONS

12/13 OVAL ROAD

LONDON NW1

30. Tampax advertisement. *Courtesy of Proctor & Gamble*

31. Advertisement for Family Planning. *Courtesy of* Woman's Weekly *1959*

almost all their annual leave to go away on what we would now regard as a proper holiday. Before that, the pattern for most couples was to have days out – again a hangover from wartime 'holidays at home'. These trips could be undertaken by bicycle or motorbike or, if one wanted to go further afield, by bus or coach. Those who lived in towns which were readily accessible to the seaside could make daily visits there if the weather was good and perhaps make use of either a family-owned or weekly rented beach hut, which gave them the security of somewhere to leave their clothes when bathing as well as offering privacy while changing instead of having to struggle discreetly into or out of a bathing costume on the beach. The well-equipped beach hut also provided a means of boiling a kettle on a small paraffin stove, but best of all it was somewhere to sit when a cold wind blew or it poured with rain.

One hazard that could be encountered on a beach in the early 1950s was the sudden emergence of either an unexploded landmine that had been buried there in the 1940s to deter enemy landing forces or a marine mine that had broken loose from its underwater mooring and been washed ashore. But such things did not deter the 1950s holidaymaker lying happily on the sands or pebbles soaking up the sun. The outward sign of a good day out at the seaside was a bright red body which, it was hoped, would turn beautifully brown once the skin had finished peeling. In our innocence we believed that the sun's rays were beneficial. We might have been warned about the dangers of sunstroke but no one really knew what that meant and, in any case, you would be all right as long as you covered your head if you were going to be in the sun all day. We had no knowledge of skin cancer or harmful UV rays, so there were no sun-blocking creams or lotions. These would come later when we ventured off to foreign parts. So with reddened backs and legs our holidaymakers made their way home to spend an uncomfortable night, eased perhaps by liberally smothering the affected areas with calamine lotion or even cold tea.

However, it was considered worth it because apart from the bathing there were other delights on offer. Most of the piers that had survived the ravages of war were now fully open for business. Some had a theatre that produced a nightly variety show throughout the summer season, often featuring a singer or comedian well known from their radio appearances. Others supported a repertory company that put on plays on a weekly or fortnightly basis. For many holidaymakers this was a rare opportunity to see a live theatrical performance. For those who liked to live dangerously there were the fun fair rides: the big wheel from the top of which you could see not only the town below but also, more exciting, the ships out at sea. After a leisurely turn on the wheel you could have your insides shaken up with a trip on the scenic railway. Then after all the excitement our couple might then wander round the stalls, she rolling pennies down little wooden chutes while he showed his prowess with a gun, shooting pellets either at a series of moving ducks or at a fixed target. At the end of the day they might take home a prize of a set of water glasses, very thick ones it's true but nonetheless a lovely reminder of a happy day out.

Those who could afford it booked themselves for a week into a seaside boarding house on a bed-and-breakfast basis. Over the years seaside landladies earned a fearsome reputation with their rigid rules and regulations. They provided, as they made very clear, only bed and breakfast; therefore you were expected to leave the house after breakfast and you were not allowed back into the house until bedtime. There were, of course, no en suite facilities, so you shared a communal bathroom that was full of notices about not hanging up wet bathing costumes or taking towels to the beach. In fact some boarding houses expected their clients to bring their own towels as well as their own soap. For those staying in a B&B the choice of activities was the same as for the day tripper, though if the area was new to them, they did have the option of exploring the town thoroughly and or visiting the surrounding area by bus or train, both of which offered 'run-about' tickets at competitive prices.

As for feeding themselves for the rest of the day, the holidaymakers most likely bought a picnic lunch and had a high tea in a café in the early evening. On the whole, the food they ate was much the same as they would have had at home. Much more hit and miss were the meals cooked over a campfire. Those keen cyclists who liked nothing better than to get away from it all into the countryside found themselves a convenient site in a friendly farmer's field to pitch their tent. They were accommodated in what was known as a ridge tent, made of heavy canvas and erected over a series of poles, the whole lot tied down with adjustable guy ropes on to metal pegs hammered into the ground. A relationship could be severely tested as a tent was put up! The 1950s couples could never have foreseen the modern lightweight, entirely weatherproof 'pop-up' tent that has separate 'rooms', not to mention space in which to stand up. Nonetheless, most campers enjoyed the experience and continued with it for years, eventually perhaps graduating to a caravan.

There were, too, other forms of camping holidays that offered much more sophistication. Holiday camps had grown up in seaside locations throughout the 1930s. Best known, though actually a latecomer to the business, was Butlins with its distinctive white-and-blue livery, but there were others to choose from, all run along the same lines. Intended as reasonably priced family holidays, the accommodation was either in individual or semi-detached wooden chalets or stone-built blocks of bedrooms. Each chalet or room contained a number of beds or bunks and basic equipment such as a chest of drawers, wardrobe and chairs. Although some also had a wash basin, lavatories and washing facilities, including showers, were provided in blocks close to the sleeping area. Landscaped lawns and gardens broke up the regimental look of the place. The main buildings housed a dining room where three substantial meals a day were served to the entire company at set times. There was a theatre for shows in the evening and dancing, and various other smaller areas for different activities such as table tennis, billiards and darts. The holiday camp idea had grown very much out of the health and beauty movement that swept through Europe in the 1930s. The aim was to provide the working population with the opportunity for healthy recreation and the emphasis was very much on enjoyment and togetherness. Consequently, from the youngest member of the family to the oldest there was something for everyone to do or a competition to join in whether it was the baby shows, children's fancy dress parades, talent shows for all ages, bathing beauty and glamorous granny contests, or the knobbly knees competition for granddad; no one need feel left out.

> *Over the years seaside landladies earned a fearsome reputation with their rigid rules and regulations*

There was something to do throughout one's waking hours. For the sports' enthusiast there was a chance to play tennis, putting, even archery and horse riding and, of course, every camp boasted a large outdoor swimming pool. Competitiveness was encouraged; on arrival holidaymakers were put into one of four houses, modelled on the system used in the public schools. Campers were encouraged to join in all the competitions during the week and their personal scores were added to those of the house. They were expected to cheer those representing their house in the football match, swimming gala or donkey derby, and at the end of the week came the grand totalling up of points and the prize-giving. So that everyone could enjoy the holiday there were crèche facilities for the very young, organised activities for the juniors throughout the day, and an evening baby-listening patrol, which gave parents the freedom to enjoy themselves, secure in the knowledge that they would be called if their child woke and was in distress. Throughout the 1950s, the holiday camp offered excellent value for money. However, like other fashions it faded somewhat when foreign package holidays became accessible, but, as is the nature of things, once the camps reorganised themselves to be more attuned to modern tastes their fortunes changed for the better.

Purely as a matter of historical interest, it should be noted that holiday camps played an unexpected role in the service of the nation. During the bitterly cold winter of 1938 at least one East Anglian holiday camp, which had closed down for the season, was reopened to accommodate those Jewish refugee children who had been brought from Germany under the Kindertransport scheme. Once war was officially declared in 1939, the army commandeered a number of holiday camps to provide temporary barracks for the troops. The other side of this was that camps established during the war were later converted into holiday camps when peace came. One such, the former base for an Auxiliary Fire Service brigade, boasted in its brochure that it had an outdoor swimming pool. The fact that the rectangular 'pool' was made of metal, had an overall depth of 6ft and was accessed by a metal ladder pointed to it having originally been the static water tank essential for firefighting.

Those couples who had no wish to spend their precious holiday time with a large number of total strangers might take advantage of family hospitality. For urban dwellers the aunt and uncle who lived in the country were the ideal relations to visit for a few days. Conversely, the rural couple would have jumped at the chance of visiting cousins in the London area. Going to stay with members of one's extended family was a custom that had existed for centuries. In the case of the 1950s couple, the 'family' might well have embraced the foster family that had taken in one or other of them as evacuees. Although we are regaled with stories of the horrors that were endured by some of those children, by far the majority found love and lasting kindness from their new family. Staying with relatives meant a comparatively cheap holiday for, although one might be expected to make a contribution to the housekeeping, there would not be any charge for accommodation. Sometimes, in country areas, help with the corn harvest, fruit picking or lifting vegetables might earn your keep while the hard work in the fresh air would most certainly do you the world of good.

Those who were more affluent might spend the whole two weeks in a smart hotel in Bournemouth or Torquay, where they would dress for dinner, which would be eaten against a background of music from a restrained string ensemble. After dinner they might make up a four to play bridge or possibly canasta, which became popular in the late 1950s. Like most of the adult population of the time they probably smoked, the men producing fine silver cigarette cases while their wives might take from their evening bags a long, elegant black cigarette holder. Into this would be fitted the tobacco that had been wrapped in perfumed pink or black paper with a gold band round the top. These cigarettes all had exotic-sounding names like Passing Cloud and Black Russian, and often came in little boxes rather than the common or garden packets manufactured by Wills, Players or Churchman. Not that the lady would have carried the whole box; she too would have a case in which to keep her cigarettes. Leaning back in her Lloyd Loom armchair in the Palm Court of the hotel, cigarette holder held at just the right angle and with a cocktail glass on the table at her side, she would have presented the picture of elegance and affluence to which many girls aspired.

However, even these folk had to return to the routine of daily life eventually. For those who wanted a taste of something different then the Continent called. There was a good train service to

Dover and then the couple would take a ferry across the Channel, followed by the train to Paris. By the end of the 1950s all that could be obtained at a reasonable price, as could a room in a hotel if one was not too fussy about its location. While some could afford to stay at the more central exclusive hotels, those who ventured into the side streets and turned a blind eye to some of the more transient occupants, found that the patron was only too willing to take them and introduce them to the owner of a nearby café where the food was not only cheap but also deliciously French. The more affluent made their way down to the Riviera, the so-called playground of the rich. One not so affluent couple on a day visit to Monte Carlo in 1957, from a resort in Italy where they were staying on a ten-day package holiday, happened to be standing outside the famous casino, wondering if they dared to enter those hallowed portals, when a familiar-looking couple emerged to stand on the steps while waiting for their car to arrive. It took a minute or two for our travellers to realise that they were looking at the Duke and Duchess of Windsor!

Isn't that what holidays are all about? Those rare, almost dream-like moments that will be remembered for years to come.

12

Health and Beauty

The introduction of the National Health Service in 1948 gave every man, woman and child in the country the right of access to all forms of medical treatment, from a simple consultation with a general practitioner to hospital treatment that might involve an expensive and intricate operation, for free. To those who had in the past paid for their medical care through a small regular payment this was wonderful news indeed. Even better was the realisation that the doctor could now also write a prescription for free medicines, tablets and medical supplies. It was not long before there was an outcry against those 'scroungers' who expected to get the simplest items like a few aspirins or a bandage for nothing. The new scheme also revolutionised the way the doctors held their surgeries. There had been a time when, if you were worried about someone's state of health, you either sent a message to the surgery – often held in part of the doctor's house – or you went to the nearest telephone box where you rang the doctor's number, reported the situation and invariably, at some time during the day, the doctor would make a visit to your home to examine the patient. However, once most people had registered with the doctor, as one was now obliged to do, the doctor had less time for home visits, which became limited to real emergencies. Instead you were expected to attend the surgery, sit on benches placed against the walls of the waiting room, beside patients suffering from all sorts of complaints. There was no appointment system, you simply turned up and waited your turn, which might take anything up to an hour to come. This gave you time to decide whether your case was as serious as you thought, especially if you found yourself in a room full of those nursing severe coughs and colds – or worse, the child who was hatching measles or chickenpox. It has also been recalled that at that time it was quite common for the waiting room to be filled with tobacco smoke.

If you decided that the wait was too long, you might decide you would self-medicate. True, this would mean you would not get your prescribed medicine free but a trip to your neighbourhood chemist, a man you trusted because you had known him for years and who had perhaps watched you grow up, could result in you getting his expert opinion on your problem plus the most suitable remedy for the complaint. The chemist might not be able to listen to your chest but he could diagnose the best form of cough mixture you required to relieve that tiresome cough. If you wanted to go it alone, then you had the pick from the shelves of such remedies as Scotts' Emulsion, Liqua Fruita (both with disgusting off-putting smells), Linctus and Lantigen B – a serious business that one, it came with a dropper to measure the liquid on to the spoon. Venos, Covonia and Owbridge's Cough Syrup were already well-established remedies. For more serious use camphorated oil, in its ribbed bottle which warned it was not for internal use, and Wintergreen ointment were popular winter standbys. So too was Vicks VapoRub, generously lathered on to the patient's chest, preferably at bedtime, and then covered with a piece of flannel; the fumes that were given off mixed with the slight tingling sensation on your skin were surprisingly comforting.

The fumes that were given off mixed with the slight tingling sensation on your skin were surprisingly comforting.

How many homes today would be able to produce a piece of flannel as they did in the 1950s? In fact how many people nowadays even know that flannel was a material, not to be confused with the piece of towelling used for a face cloth also known as a flannel? In late Victorian times it was believed that garments of thick red flannel worn next to the skin would induce good health. In the mid-1850s a mother was advised that her sickly baby daughter would live to adulthood only if she always wore red flannel. There must have been something in the belief because her daughter lived until just before her 100th birthday! And, of course, we all know from E. Nesbit's *The Railway Children* just how useful a red flannel petticoat can be in emergencies. In the 1950s when a doctor prescribed the use of a kaolin poultice, he would assume that there would be flannel in the house on which to spread it.

The 1950s housewife would have known that when her husband had a bad cold that involved severely congested nasal passages then the answer was to purchase a bottle of Friar's Balsam. Filling a bowl (often her yellow mixing bowl from the kitchen) with boiling water into which she placed a few drops of the powerful yellow mixture, she would persuade her invalid to sit with his head over the steaming bowl while she used a large towel to make a sort of tent over his head so that he could clear the congestion by inhaling the strong fumes that rose up. Incidentally, the concentrated steaming was also good for opening the pores on the face if one happened to suffer with blackheads. The early 1950s housewife was also likely to treat a stye with Golden Eye ointment, and use zinc and castor oil ointment for rashes and boracic ointment for cuts and grazes. Germolene was also used for the latter purpose, although Dettol and TCP were far more fashionable, if more expensive, than common old salt and water for cleansing wounds, and less painful than iodine.

In the war years most families had kept a stock of old sheeting for home emergencies, and thin strips were torn off and rolled up ready to make bandages. In the days before sticky tape was in general use it was usual to split the end of the sheeting bandage down to the required length to make a self-tie. But by the 1950s, there were ample stocks not only of lint, which was placed over a wound, but proper bandages too, and sticking plasters which could supplant the use of the gauze bandages. The adhesive quality of these fabric plasters was much stronger than the later plasticised ones, as anyone who had one ripped off could testify. Removal by ripping intensified but shortened the pain.

If one can judge an age by the advertisements that appeared in the press and magazines, then the 1950s, like previous generations, was obsessed with its bowels. In those days, regardless of the reason for a visit to the doctor, he always did two things: first he asked you to stick your tongue out and then he enquired if your bowels were all right. As one automatically replied yes to this, one never found out exactly what this 'all right' meant. The importance of 'keeping regular' was so ingrained in the national psyche that mothers would automatically dose their children weekly with syrup of figs, usually after the Friday or Saturday night bath. Adults also took laxatives in varying forms – Epsom salts in a little hot water before your morning cup of tea was common amongst men, though younger men preferred the gentle effervescence of Andrews Liver Salt, Enos Fruit Salts or Alka Seltzer. All these were supposed to give 'inner cleanliness'. For those who needed more drastic treatment there were the dreaded castor oil, liquid paraffin and senna pods. The 1950s housewife, however, was more likely to opt for the much-advertised Bile Beans, which, in an advertisement of 1953, stated that their role was the 'breaking up and gently disposing of fats and other harmful residue'. Sold in tiny round boxes these little yellow-coated pills were also marketed as 'keeping you Healthy, Bright-eyed and Slim'. Although she might claim that she needed the nightly pill to aid her digestion, help her constipation or soothe her menstrual problems, many young women were discreetly induced to take the pills as an aid to slimming. It's odd that, with the word, bile in their title, these pills ever caught on, but they were successful worldwide. Funnily enough, the makers of Carter's Little Liver Pills, which were similar, were advised to drop the word 'liver' from their advertising. While Bile Beans no longer exist, their rival pills from Beechams, 'worth a guinea a box', were only discontinued in 1998, while their powders in many forms have continued as remedies for various ills.

The desire of women to be slim and youthful is nothing new – however far back in time one cares to go, you will find a method that was supposed to achieve miracles. In the 1950s advertisements appeared in women's magazines under the banner 'Figure it out' accompanied by a line drawing of an elegant woman in a smart suit and wearing a close-fitting hat adorned with two large feathers, one hand on her slim waist, the other on the head of a dog of the retriever type. The text read:

> You ARE young when you feel young … you feel young when
> you LOOK young. Zest, poise, vitality – all the gaiety of a happy,
> full life – these make up the charm of the woman who preserves
> the girlish lines of youth.

How did one achieve this? By taking Marmola brand anti-fat
tablets. At 3s 8½d a box, these were quite expensive. Like most
of the articles of this type that appeared in advertisements they
were available from the chemist's or by post, so that they could be
acquired discreetly.

Perhaps one of the oddest aids to shedding weight appeared
during the second half of the 1950s in the shape, no pun intended,
of Stephanie Bowman slimming garments. The term garment was
somewhat misleading for what in fact amounted to a series of
pink plastic bags with elasticated tops and bottoms. Working on
the principle of a Turkish bath, the idea was that you could reduce
certain areas of your body by encasing the part – thighs and upper
arms in particular – in one of the bags and then wearing one's
clothes over the top either all night or during the day. The resulting
sweat was supposed to start the slimming process.

If our housewives visited the doctor following a bout of flu or
a persistent cough, they were likely to tell him that they felt 'run
down'. The remedy for this state was a prescription for a bottle of
'tonic', usually a thick black concoction that tasted vile. The medical
profession seemed to work on the assumption that the worse it
tasted the more good it did you. Far more pleasant were tonic wines
such as Sanatogen and Wincarnis purchased from the off-licence.
These naturally were comparatively expensive but a concerned
mother was likely to buy her daughter a bottle if she thought it
would improve her health. Some doctors bypassed the tonic wine
option and actually suggested the taking of a good red burgundy if
a woman was thought to be anaemic, or even a daily glass of stout
for a nursing mother.

For the occasional headache or stomach cramps the 1950s
housewife would have taken Aspros, which were sold individually
encased in strips of pink paper. Phensic, which was advertised as
being better than aspirin alone, was also popular, and was offered
as a remedy for a variety of ailments including rheumatic pains,

while by the middle to end of the decade both codeine and Anadin tablets were on the market. Codeine was used widely in a number of medicines for its analgesic qualities but its use was eventually curtailed when its addictive quality was recognised. During the 1950s great strides were made in the pharmaceutical industry that led to the introduction of tablets being used in various treatments; two important ones were penicillin and the mysteriously named M & B tablets. You knew you had something rather special if the doctor said, 'I'll put you on M & B'. But on the whole, certainly during the early part of the decade, most people who visited the doctor expected to receive what was known in some parts of the country as 'a bottle'. We have already referred to the tonic but other medicines were dispensed in large clear glass bottles. Often these coloured concoctions, which might be bright red, yellow or dark brown, were to be diluted in a small quantity of water or taken directly from the teaspoon, usually three times a day. Some were heavily sweetened to disguise the taste while others smelled as foul as they tasted.

You knew you had something rather special if the doctor said, 'I'll put you on M & B'

Since we have just toured the chemist's shop and in passing have mentioned menstruation, which was rarely mentioned publicly, this seems the appropriate place to talk of the sanitary products available in the 1950s. Bulky sanitary towels, packed by the dozen in almost plain wrappers were purchased either from an old-fashioned drapery shop or from the chemist. For the young woman it was embarrassing to have to ask the male chemist for a packet of Lilia or Silcot. Their advertising, which said 'She's fastidious! She does not take just anything. She knows the towel which gives her the greatest comfort and she carefully asks for it time after time', certainly did not apply to the girl who would rather wait until the female assistant was on duty or alternatively go to another shop where she wasn't known. In the 1950s it was a brave unmarried woman who dared to ask for a packet of Tampax or Lillets. Where nowadays our 5-year-olds see and hear advertisements for such things, the Tampax advertisement that appeared in a magazine of July 1951 seems to belong almost to the Victorian era. As the bold type declared:

I Bless The Day I Wrote For It
It's odd how one simple action can bring
such long-lasting benefits! Many and
many women, hearing some modern-
minded friend praising Tampax, has
sent for a sample, and found an amazing
difference in her life. Undreamed of
comfort. Simplicity in use. Such
tremendous advantages over old-
fashioned methods. And such security!

A Confidential Trial
If you are modern-minded enough to
test the extra-daintiness, comfort and
peace of mind that Tampax brings, do
so *in confidence*. Just send sixpence in
stamps to The Nurse, Dept, 174,
Tampax Ltd.,......................
for a trial packet in plain
cover, with fully informative literature.
You too may bless the day.

This really is a minor masterpiece of advertising copy. It is eye-catching with its simple outline drawing of an elegantly dressed young woman standing behind a small table with a bowl of flowers and a book on it, which immediately suggests she is both discerning and intelligent. There is a play on the fact that using Tampax is something one's friends do, thus implying you are being left behind – you are not a modern woman. At the same time there is the comforting reassurance that 'The Nurse' will receive your request, and even more reassuring is the note that your free trial pack will be sent in plain packaging in other words no one else picking up the post from the mat will know what the packet contains.

It would appear that the company had to overcome a certain amount of resistance and reluctance to use their product. For many women there was a fear that they might somehow harm themselves by using internal protection, while it was believed by some that it was impossible for an unmarried woman – that is, a presumed virgin – to be capable of using them. It often took an enlightened female PE teacher to explain that school gymnastics had taken care of that particular concern. So we find that by the middle of the decade, Tampax's advertising was far more direct than that quoted above. Among a list of FACTS, it included the one that the tampons were suitable for use by *every* woman.

One thing has become apparent during the last fifty years and that is that the longer we live, the younger we seem to remain. For a start, women are no longer expected to 'dress their age', whatever that means, but there was a time when fashions were produced with certain age groups in mind. Designers for the mass market produced garments that were aimed at the younger woman, 'the junior Miss', who was about to start work, and those in their 20s; next came the more mature woman, and by the time you had reached 50 you were expected to settle for what can only be described as downright dowdy clothes. Think Ena Sharples and her friends. Similarly, clothes were sized: 'W' (Women), 'WX' (Women's Extra) and 'OS' (Outsize). Manufacturers tended to assume that as women aged so they expanded in size, so the more stylish dresses were in W size and the more matronly were WX or OS. This was extremely hard on the young woman who was not stock size and was forced to find something to fit her from the outsize range. There were few words more humiliating than 'I'm afraid we have nothing in your size, Madam!' On the subject of sizing, while today we have some women striving to achieve a one-digit size, others are much bigger than they were in the 1950s. The knitting patterns of the era were for a standard bust size of 34/5in and 36/7in. Only occasionally did they extend as far as the larger size of 39/40.

As we have moved on in so many directions, and nowadays are accustomed to svelte septuagenarian film actresses advertising the need to keep our skin young looking, it is surprising to find an advertisement from 1952 which exhorts us 'After 25 – Watch for Dry Skin', and then goes on to tell us:

Round about the age of 25, every woman should use her mirror with a more critical eye. Tiny lines, flakiness, dry patches – these show that the natural oils of the skin are beginning to decrease. Before 40, skin may lose as much as 20% of its own softening oil. A special new cream, Pond's Dry Skin Cream, offsets this inevitable drying out. Three features make Pond's Dry Skin Cream so effective. 1. It is rich in lanolin, very like the skin's natural oil. 2. It is homogenised to soak in better. 3. It has a softening emulsifier.

It is interesting that the advertisement makes the point that the cream uses a natural product and, unlike a modern advertisement, it does not blind the potential user with long-winded scientific terms, though 'homogenised' was not in most people's vocabulary at the time. Also unlike a modern advertisement, the makers do not suggest that the problem should be tackled by using a day and a night cream; instead this Dry Skin Cream can be used at all times and all for the very reasonable price of 2s 9d a jar (the same price of a good seat in the balcony of the cinema). Another difference we should note is that the recommendation 'Pond's Dry Skin Cream is really remarkable. It is so very rich – yet very soft, too – and never sticky. I like it better than any other', came not from a cinematic or stage celebrity but Lady Daphne Straight, a member of the aristocracy, the daughter of an earl.

Pond's had held the market in face cream for a long time; many a school child had been mystified by the advertisement for its Vanishing Cream. One can almost imagine Richmal Crompton's Just William getting hold of his sister Ethel's jar to put it to the test. Certainly most 1950s housewives would have started using it, even if in time they moved on to other products. But it was inexpensive and had a proven record, and was a good base for the requisite application of face powder. An essential item in every woman's handbag was her powder compact. A girl knew that she had truly reached womanhood when she was presented with one of these; often given as a really expensive 21st birthday present. Varying in shape as well as material, invariably the design on the lid was inlaid with painted or enamel flowers or birds. Inside the lid was a mirror, then came the small powder puff, beneath which was the insert through which the powder was filtered. In those days loose face powder was sold in small round boxes from which one filled the compact. In many ways this was both messy and time consuming, so the arrival of compressed powder refills was warmly welcomed.

Then came pancake make-up introduced by Max Factor, as an offshoot of that used in films. Eyeshadow and eyebrow pencils were used to highlight the eyes, while the rouge that mother had used was definitely consigned to the back of the dressing table drawer. The introduction of pale shimmering pink for both lipstick and nail varnish widened the customer base as many young women whose parents and later husbands had believed that bright red lips and nails were not for the likes of them dared to try the pinks.

It is difficult nowadays to imagine what it was like before the days of self-service in practically every store. With counters and display cases manned by assistants, one really needed to know what it was you wanted to purchase. Fortunately, for Miss and Mrs Average, there was always Woolworths, which kept a good range of cosmetics on show as well as reasonably priced perfumes, the most popular of which was Bourjois Evening in Paris, with its distinctive dark blue bottles and packaging.

Ladies in the past had kept cut-glass, silver-topped bowls on their dressing tables filled with dusting powder but by the 1950s the perfume makers were producing fancy tins of talcum powder available to every woman. These tins, teamed up with perfumed soap (now no longer rationed), and placed in a fancy box became ideal Christmas gifts. Often the box also contained either a bottle of coloured bath salts (scented washing-soda crystals) or half a dozen bath cubes. These squares, about the size of four Oxo cubes, wrapped in silver paper with an outer wrapper that declared what scent they were, were crumbled – just like the Oxo or a Symington's soup cube – into one's bath. Bath salts were also sold loose by weight and the enterprising woman could practice both economy and recycling by filling jam jars, which she had previously decorated, with the bath crystals. For a few pence and a little time and skill, she had achieved several presents for female family and friends.

Towards the end of the 1950s, we were becoming much more concerned about how we smelled – or didn't, as the case might be. The makers of Lifebuoy soap had made us all aware of its power to remove body odour, and advertisements began to appear suggesting that it was the duty of a best friend not to shirk telling one the truth. Although there was an old saying that 'horses sweat, gentlemen perspire and ladies glow', our housewives too were now regularly using underarm deodorants. To begin with, some of these came in liquid form, like Odo-o-no, or as a cream, like Arrid, before developing into roll-ons and aerosol spray anti-perspirants. If they could stand the smell housewives were also removing the hair on their legs and underarms with Veet – a practice best done when husbands were out of the house.

For the girls who as children had cleaned their teeth after rubbing a dampened tooth brush on the little solid pink block known as dentifrice, manufactured by Gibbs and sold in small red tins bearing what we would now call a logo of little ivory towers, there was now not only a choice of toothpaste but mouth-washes too to make sure that their breath was always 'fresh'. Which brings us to the question – whatever happened to chlorophyll? To most people today, this term is applied to the natural process in plants of the photosynthesis of sunlight, which gives them their green colour. I can

Towards the end of the 1950s, we were becoming much more concerned about how we smelled - or didn't, as the case might be.

still recall a school visit to a local manufactory of chlorophyll and the indescribable smell that emanated from the huge vats in which the natural chemical was extracted. Suddenly, in the 1950s, the market was flooded with products, including toothpaste, that contained this chlorophyll. The rather earthy green compound was even turned into tablets that were supposed to provide that 'fresh breath'. So successful was the advertising for these tablets that they were bought mainly by men.

The great beauty debate that has raged for generations of whether or not to wash one's face with soap and water was still going on in the 1950s even though by then toilet soap no longer contained the harsh elements of the past. Lux, for example, boasted of its purity and gentleness upon the skin, as did other well-known brands such as Imperial Leather and Palmolive. But this was the era when products appeared on the market that proved just how useless soap and water were in cleansing the skin. One lotion instructed you to dab it all over the face and then remove it bit by bit with small pads of cotton wool. When one saw the dirt that was removed, it would be months, if ever, before one reverted to soap and water. This was also the era of blackheads that needed to be steamed and gently squeezed to remove them. And, of course, there was always the face pack – preferably one that contained yeast. It was essential that the young housewife had time and privacy to plaster her face with the white mixture which not only caused all the pores in the face to open but, when it set hard, was supposed to tighten all one's facial muscles. Absolute stillness was required during this treatment; woe betide anyone who disturbed the recipient, causing the mask to crack. Once it was well and truly set, then came the messy operation of washing it all off. Then it was time to lie down and relax with a slice of cucumber placed on each eyelid.

The 1950s housewife would have been very keen to maintain a healthy weight. Her lifestyle was such that she took plenty of exercise without even thinking about it. She automatically walked daily to the shops to buy fresh food, or to work; or, if the latter was several miles away, she would cycle. Her work within the house also involved more energy than the modern housewife expends. Laundry done by hand involved filling bowls or tubs, rubbing the items, wringing the garments and finally walking out with the laundry basket to the garden and hanging it out on the line. It would make an interesting energy comparison with that and the filling of a washing machine and emptying of a tumble drier. Similarly, not everyone had a vacuum cleaner so floors were swept and polished, carpets brushed and kitchen floors scrubbed. Windows were regularly cleaned inside and out, though fortunately the disappearance of sash windows brought an end to the practice of the housewife sitting on the window sill to clean the outside of upper-storey windows. Many women continued to play tennis or netball, while the popular Saturday night dance still provided splendid exercise. And, of course, there was always the gardening to be done.

The 1950s woman had grown up accustomed to the limited diet enforced by rationing, thus she had not been able to indulge a 'sweet tooth' with a never-ending supply of confectionery, cakes and biscuits. Both finance and the routine of three meals a day with the occasional treat conditioned what she ate. But, of course, there were some who thought they needed to lose weight, and these women were advised to follow a regime that cut out carbohydrates, which in those days meant bread and potatoes. The more recent cabbage soup diet was preceded by that of the cauliflower, where the cooking liquor was drunk first, the cauliflower head forming the main meal. In the 1930s the very popular Hay Diet had not only forbidden carbohydrates, but had decreed that proteins and vegetables should never be mixed at a meal. A variation of that diet appeared during the mid-1950s in a women's magazine under the title of 'The Two by Two Diet'. After two days of starvation to clear the system, the would-be slimmer launched herself into a routine of eating (for however long was necessary) only protein foods for two days, alternating with fruit and vegetables on the next two days. If anything, the latter was the easier to manage as one could feel quite full on a plate of mixed salad followed by chopped fruit. An unaccompanied lump of cheese or a piece of chicken just didn't seem to satisfy the eye, let alone the stomach. But the regime did seem to achieve a satisfactory weight loss as well as a general improvement in one's skin.

Ryvita had appeared in the 1930s, introducing the nation to a crisp bread made of rye as an alternative to soft bread made of wheat. Although not originally intended as a slimming product it became so during the 1950s. It certainly was more versatile and appetising than the specifically designed diet food, which included the Energen range. The rather expensive Energen rolls that attempted to masquerade as bread rolls took the form of balls of cellulose with added gluten. Originally meant for diabetics, it was boasted that they were delicious cut in half and spread with margarine and a scrape of jam, but they tasted of cotton wool! If you were a slimmer, better to go without than have a mouthful of cellulose.

Bathroom scales were not in general use in the 1950s, so if one was trying to watch one's weight, it was necessary to use the scales in your local chemist's shop. The most accurate were those where weights were moved across a beam placed in front of you. To get a really accurate reading, you needed the chemist or his assistant to move the weights along the beam. If, however, you did not wish to reveal your weight to anyone else, then you could, for the price of one penny in the slot, be weighed by standing on a small platform, and your weight would be recorded on the dial in front of you. If you were a glutton for punishment, then you took your penny to Woolworths and stood on the scales, which were usually situated just inside the main entrance. This gigantic red machine had an enormous dial and once you stood on the platform your weight was revealed to the world at large.

While on the subject of placing pennies in the slot, in the 1950s the now euphemistic term for visiting the lavatory really did mean spending a penny. Perhaps we can include this under the heading of health – that is, public health. In the 1950s every town had a number of public lavatories placed at regular intervals to ensure that one was never far from a convenience. Often these were placed in or near bus stations or trolley bus termini and were situated below ground where they might also provide an area where parcels could be left while doing one's shopping. Male and female facilities were rarely placed side by side; they were situated instead at a discreet distance. In the majority of cases, the lavatories were supervised by attendants, who took a pride in keeping their domain spotless. Not only were the cubicles kept clean and polished but, in those days when the water supply to the overhead cisterns was carried in copper pipes, these glowed like beacons, betokening the attendant's pride in his or her work. Each cubicle had a slot machine on its door and it was into this that you placed your penny. Some conveniences had one cubicle tucked away that was free, for the use of those who were needy. However, something which would appal today's health and safety inspectors was that in those days there were no general hand-washing facilities. You could, if you wished, pay sixpence for what was called a wash and brush up. The lavatory attendant would take your money and provide you with some soap and a towel, then admit you to an inner sanctum beyond a glass door. Here there were several washbasins that provided hot water. There was also a mirror for the lady to repair her make-up. A small but prominent little dish on the attendant's table, which might include another with safety pins or a needle and thread, indicated that a small tip would be appreciated.

Some councils decided to dispense with the penny in the slot on the cubicle doors and instead installed turnstiles at the entrance into which the penny was inserted. This was often a reaction to beat the petty criminals who attempted to break open the machine on the cubicle door. It was also intended as a deterrent to those who delighted in writing rhymes and messages on the cubicle walls or who used unsupervised lavatories as a meeting place. However, turnstiles caused very serious problems for some members of the public. The first was that you had to have the requisite coin for the slot. With the old method, the attendant was able to give you change. With a turnstile, a desperate person might have to wait for some time to find another prospective user who would either give them a penny or change the larger coin. There was a joke at the time that the definition of a gentleman was one who, when asked for a penny, did not give two halfpennies. But the biggest drawback to the turnstile for women involved size. To start with a mother with a baby in a pushchair was unable to get that through; if she had a toddler there could be problems trying to squeeze the child through with her. The heavy iron framework was enough to frighten a small child from ever using one again. Elderly and disabled women also had problems, but those who suffered most were those who did not conform to the size allocated by the mechanism to allow entry. By the late 1950s the plight of all women in the use of turnstiles was discussed at great length in parliament, the cause being taken up initially by Barbara Castle, backed by the larger-than-life MP Bessie Braddock. Finally, in 1963, turnstiles in public lavatories provided by local authorities were made illegal.

13

The Status of Women in the 1950s

The official view of the status of married women in the 1950s is summed up neatly in the word 'housewife'. After the war, when demobilised servicemen returned to take up their old work, women were no longer needed to do the jobs they had held down during the men's absence and the powers that be decided that one of the ways to deal with this and build a new, better Britain was by creating the nuclear family with the wife/mother set securely in the centre of the home, rather as the middle classes had done in late Victorian times. Worthy though this idea might be, it generated an attitude in many workplaces that since young women employees were not likely to stay long in a job once they were married, because inevitably they would start a family, it was not worth giving them any extra training that would set them on the path to a successful career. Carrying this policy to its logical conclusion meant that many women who remained unmarried, or married but childless, were denied the opportunities for promotion they should have had. To combat this prejudice young engaged women in teacher-training colleges were often warned they should not wear their rings when attending an interview for a post. However, in those pre-'politically correct days', the governing body and members of the interview panel could ask any questions they liked, even if it did come occasionally dressed up in the euphemism of the gentleman who asked a candidate, 'Miss ..., are you, um, so to speak, heart-whole and fancy free?' Worse perhaps, was the interview panel who turned down a well-qualified candidate for a head of department position on the grounds that, newly married at the ripe old age of 30, she would be bound to start a family almost immediately.

Books, magazines, films and, later, television programmes tried hard to reinforce the idyllic picture of the perfect stay-at-home housewife who took care of the home, raised the children, cooked nutritious meals, and provided a haven of calm for her hardworking husband when he returned at the end of his working day. The romantic novelist Barbara Cartland was often to be heard on the wireless dispensing advice on how the good wife should prepare herself to greet her husband, not only with a delicious meal prepared but herself bathed, perfumed and dressed in smart clean clothes, complete with fresh frilly apron, ready to spend a cosy and possibly romantic evening with him. One wonders how many frazzled women were tempted to throw something at the radio after they had spent the day wrestling with a fractious, teething baby and a 2-year-old's tantrums, not to mention the broken washing line that had trailed all the clean nappies in the flowerbeds. They would, of course, have their husband's evening meal ready but it was doubtful if they would have had the time to run a comb through their hair, let alone wash their face and apply make-up. The women who might take Miss Cartland's advice or heed that given in magazines were those who most probably had some help in the house. If all your washing went to the laundry from whence everything, including your husband's shirts, returned beautifully ironed, and if you had an obliging Mrs Mopp who came, perhaps not every day but certainly more than once a week, to scrub, clean and polish, then like Mrs Dale whose diary was broadcast daily, you too could strive to be the perfect housewife.

However, the reality for most women was very different. Most of the young couples who married during the 1950s relied on saving the wife's weekly wage towards furnishing their home, or providing necessities for when they started a family. The younger the husband the more likely he was to accept that his wife worked, and often he was prepared to share the household chores with her. Older husbands were more entrenched in their outlook – as, it would seem, were some of those who lived in the countryside. These were likely to adopt the attitude of, 'No wife of mine is going out to work!' Whether this was from fear that other people would think him incapable of providing adequately for her or an unconscious desire to retain his control of her is not clear. The wife who remained at home was wholly dependent on her husband for money. If one belonged to the more affluent parts of society then the husband might make his wife a monthly allowance for her own personal use – no questions asked. He would probably also take responsibility for all the household bills. On the other hand, the majority of stay-at-home wives were given a sum from their husband's weekly pay packet and were expected to run the house, and feed and clothe themselves and later the children, out of it. In some households the man handed over his unopened pay packet to his wife who then gave him back what amounted to his pocket money. Others allotted varying amounts into tins or jars to cover the rent, bills for the utilities, insurance policies or to pay the regular instalments on essential items, such as the gas or electric cooker, bought on a hire-purchase agreement. Another receptacle was earmarked for storing the one-, later two-shilling pieces needed to feed the gas and electricity meters if that method of payment was used.

It is hardly surprising that during the 1950s feminism was bubbling away below the surface.

The most haphazard of all these financial arrangements was the one where the husband placed his wages in a disused teapot or caddy on the mantelpiece, most usually, or on the top shelf of the kitchen cupboard. This 'bank' was then drawn on when needed but it was a method that relied on great trust that neither party would be tempted to overspend on some non-essential item. Most stay-at-home wives had a set amount given to them that was considered sufficient to buy the weekly food supplies. Whichever system was adopted, it was left to the housewife to squirrel away what she could, to cover such items as make-up, a rare visit to the hairdresser, or birthday and Christmas presents. When asked if he could remember how much housekeeping money his wife had when they married in the 1950s, a gentleman expostulated: 'I never gave her any, I paid everything!' He then added, 'she never wanted for anything, she only had to ask!' And that sums up the position of the majority of the stay-at-home housewives of the 1950s – total financial dependency upon their husbands.

This dependency or being viewed merely as an adjunct to one's husband overlapped into other areas. For a married woman who also worked, there was nothing more annoying, when faced with an official form that required the answer to the question 'occupation' to be instructed by the official on the other side of the desk or counter, to write 'housewife'. And worse, being told that you needed your husband's permission, verified by his signature, to do certain things, such as enter into a hire-purchase agreement. It was assumed that a woman might default on payments, unless they were backed by her husband. A wife's salary, however large it was, could not, for example, be counted towards a mortgage. However, unmarried women with a decent salary were able to obtain a mortgage provided it was adequately backed by a life insurance policy. One woman who had been in this position found herself treated very differently several years later when she married. As a single woman she had been able to sign legal documents and was considered intelligent enough both to understand and negotiate with builders, agents and solicitors. But as a married woman things were very different; every little detail had to be passed and signed for by her new husband, which, as he was often working away, could prove difficult. Most galling was the condescending way she was now treated by the men in suits. Suddenly she had become stereotyped as the 'little woman', a mere housewife, incapable of understanding things in the 'man's world'. It is hardly surprising that during the 1950s feminism was bubbling away below the surface.

One fight that was on going during the 1950s was for equal pay for women and men doing the same or similar jobs. Women teachers and civil servants achieved parity by the end of the 1950s but other employers took much more convincing and women continued to be paid less than their male counterparts. Similarly, women were still not readily accepted in what were considered male professions. The first woman bank manager was appointed in 1958 but I am reliably informed that even after this momentous event, many older managers refused to appoint female counter assistants in their branch of the bank. Worse perhaps than this chauvinistic attitude on the part of the manager was the hostility of some of the male customers who, when women did appear behind the counter, refused to be served by them and would deliberately move to a counter served by a male. It would be interesting to know the reasoning behind this. It surely can't have been the fear that women could not be trusted with figures since women undertook the book-keeping in most offices. Yet fear of women there must have been because it is reported that many of the long-established managers did not even feel comfortable interviewing female customers without their husbands being present. It would seem that the character of Captain Mainwaring of *Dad's Army* really was based on a typical bank manager of the time. If it was hard for some men to accept women working in banks, how much more tenacity would a bright girl who wanted to be an engineer need; first to persuade her teachers so that she could study the right subjects to gain the relevant place at university and, having gained that place, often with great difficulty, and then achieved a good degree, to find an engineering company that would take her on. Slowly, slowly, graduates in mathematics and all the sciences broke down barriers and opened the way for others, but very often not without a fight for acceptance and equality.

However, as much as the post-war government wanted to create a Utopia peopled with happy families with the man as the breadwinner and his wife doing her duty by looking after the home he had provided for her, rearing his children and fulfilling his physical needs in return for being kept, those in high places seemed unaware of the realities. The war had had many far-reaching effects but one of the greatest was in breaking up what had appeared to be the norm for family life. The prospect of invasion by the enemy in 1939 had uprooted thousands of children from their homes in vulnerable areas. Those of school age were evacuated en masse with their schools to towns and villages throughout the country. Urban children from overcrowded streets suddenly found themselves surrounded by fields and unfamiliar animals, living with people who spoke a different language, or so it seemed to the Cockney suddenly transported to Devon. Other children went even further afield, crossing oceans to stay with friends or relations in Canada, the United States and Australasia. The adolescents and young adults who returned home five or six years later often came back as products of an entirely different culture to that of their parents, who were now strangers.

Many of the men who had been in the services and survived the war also returned to their wives as virtual strangers. Even those who had managed regular leave had, in the main, lived an entirely separate life from their families for the duration of the war. Inevitably, some would have found it difficult to remain faithful to their wives at home and would have sought companionship and intimacy with the women who lived near their billets. A harmless invitation to join a civilian family for tea on Sunday, which the YMCA canteens encouraged locals to offer, might lead to an affair. But that was probably all right, provided it was kept quiet, because, as everyone knew, men had needs. It was quite a different story if a wife was discovered 'carrying on', perhaps with a workmate in the factory or office or a lonely serviceman. Women were supposed to be pure and chaste – no one ever mentioned their needs – the only problem was that where the man could walk away from his entanglements, a woman was sometimes literally left holding the baby.

If this happened, and there was no way the wife could pretend her husband was the father, then he had one of the few grounds for divorce that were available at that time. Again, it was a class thing. Readers of the Sunday newspapers were kept abreast of the activities of those in the higher echelons of society whose marriages were dissolved, often involving large financial settlements. American film stars also went off to the city of Reno where, according to the gossip columns, it was possible to get a 'quickie' divorce that would enable a new marriage to take place shortly afterwards. But divorce was not for ordinary people, not only because of the legal costs involved but also because of the stigma that accompanied such action. If a partner was found to have committed adultery then dissolution of the marriage might be considered. But, mainly because of the financial implications, it was more likely that a man would sue on the grounds of his wife's adultery than that she would take action against him, even if he was a serial adulterer. As the wife was financially dependent on her husband she was not in a position to leave the marital home and take the children with her, so many women stayed in abusive or utterly dead relationships because there was no alternative.

Amongst the more enlightened in government and elsewhere, there was an acknowledgement that the whole question of divorce needed modernising, so, in 1951, a Royal Commission was set up to consider a change in the laws which permitted divorce only on the grounds of matrimonial fault – adultery, cruelty – or desertion of three or more years. It was argued that marriage should no longer be regarded as a binding legal duty but rather a companionate union, and therefore if the relationship of love and affection broke down it should be terminated. It was also proposed that those who had lived apart for seven years should be granted a divorce without question. In 1956 there was a further Royal Commission on both marriage and divorce. This one recognised that many of our accepted standards had altered:

> [It has to be accepted] … that greater demands are now made of marriage, consequent on the spread of education, higher standards of living and the social and economic emancipation of women … Old restraints, such as social penalties on sexual relations outside marriage, have weakened … [and there is] a tendency to regard the assertion of one's own individuality as a right and to pursue one's personal satisfaction, reckless of the consequences to others … There is a tendency to take the duties and responsibilities of marriage less seriously than formerly.

It is interesting to see that what, sixty years later, has been dubbed as the 'Me' generation obviously had its seeds in the 1950s. Recognising that life had changed was one thing but taking action was another. The Commission and the government still saw marriage as an institution not a relationship. Therefore adultery was an offence against an institution, which harmed the moral and social fabric of society. Thus the wrongdoer should be punished. So strongly did they feel on the subject they actually considered abolishing divorce altogether. Better, they believed, to educate the nation on the duties and responsibilities of marriage – something they are still talking about in the second decade of the twenty-first century. So nothing further was done to help those who wished to extricate themselves from difficult marriages until the matter came up again for review in the 1960s. Thus a number of women had to endure not only the torment of a loveless marriage but also had to put up with the disapproval of their parents and families at the very mention of a divorce – to their parents this spoke of social stigma that in some way reflected upon them. 'What will the neighbours say' was often heard – and used as a threat too in an attempt to bring a recalcitrant daughter to her senses. Early twenty-first-century folk may sometimes bewail the loss of community spirit and neighbourliness, but if the opinion of the neighbours was so important that a life could be ruined then perhaps the modern way is not quite so bad after all.

Many women gave up their own ambitions for a good career and took less fulfilling jobs merely to earn money that would help them while their husbands were studying. There were those young men who had left school at 15, gone to work and then been conscripted to do their two years' National Service, who discovered that they had no wish to return to their previous dead-end employment but wished instead to better their chances in life. Some chose to follow a different career path entirely, which would require additional study to achieve their aim. Thousands of young wives supported their husbands financially as they attended short-term college courses, while for those undertaking home-study or evening courses, the additional expense of textbooks and fees was drawn from the wife's pay packet. Times were indeed hard for these couples but the experience seems to have strengthened rather than weakened their relationships.

> *Adultery was an offence against an institution, which harmed the moral and social fabric of society.*

14

'Fings Ain't Wot They Used T'be

There is no doubt that the 1950s put in train many of the changes which shaped the way we now live our lives. The rejection of established ideas on individual and social conduct, the blurring of class barriers, the desire for equality and the expectation of a higher standard of living, have all had varying effects as, over the last sixty years, taboo after taboo from the past has been broken down. For the benefit of those who don't recognise the heading above (and may think that it is merely indicative of the decline in the use of Standard English), it was the title of a highly successful play by the young playwright Frank Norman, with music by Lionel Bart, that was first produced in 1959 by Joan Littlewood at the experimental Theatre Royal Stratford, London. This Cockney play followed others of the early 1950s that dealt with the lives of the working classes in a way that had not been seen since Arnold Bennett. Much of the drama of the 1950s was exhilarating and thought provoking; one came away from a night at the theatre not so much entertained as full of unanswered questions that nagged at your brain for weeks. The best example of this was Samuel Becket's *Waiting for Godot*. West End theatres flourished, offering a wide diversity of plays to suit all tastes, but, best of all, the tickets were affordable. If one was prepared to sit high up, right at the back of the theatre in what was known as the 'gods' on a hard wooden bench rather than an individual seat, then one could see top-quality plays for as little as 1s or 2s. Many young people were also introduced to a lifelong love of ballet and opera from a seat in the 'gods' at Sadlers Wells.

It was thinking about this accessibility to certain things in the 1950s that started the train of thought about those things that are either 'not what they used to be' or have faded into insignificance. What came immediately to mind was the change in communications. When she married in the 1950s, the chances were that the bride moved away from the town or village where she had grown up. If she was particularly close to her parents and siblings then she would want to keep in close contact with them. Depending on the distance involved it was possible that they might exchange weekly visits. Often the newlyweds would be invited to Sunday lunch or tea at the parental home, a practice that quickly developed into a habit that after some time could prove to be restrictive. On the other hand, if such visits were not possible then the only way to maintain contact for most people was by writing a letter. This exchange of letters was highly valued by both parties. Each writer expressed in their own unique style an account of their activities, the gossip about family and friends, as well as sometimes pouring out worries about money, relationships or health. The most important thing about a letter was that it could be kept and re-read several times over so that every detail was absorbed. It also provided reference points for the return letter. For people like Diana far away in Nigeria, letters from home must have been very welcome while hers to her parents would have given reassurance. They would have been able to use the thin blue air letter which one bought at the post office for sixpence. That gave you a good page and a half of space and took far less time to reach its destination than a letter that went by sea. Whoever you were and wherever you lived, letter writing would have been a very important part of your life in the 1950s. Many very ordinary people still keep sixty- or seventy-year-old letters that can bring back the 'voice' of a loved one now gone. Letters also often revealed the true feelings of a person that they would never have uttered in a face-to-face conversation. An email or a text message does not have the same depth of feeling – and both can so easily be erased.

There was much to be said for the postal service in those days with its twice-daily deliveries to every urban house and several collections throughout the day, until quite late in the evening, from strategically placed pillar boxes. Most letters posted one day were delivered on the following one, so it was possible to arrange to meet someone at fairly short notice. The postcard, which carried a lower postage charge, was particularly useful for this purpose. In case of a real emergency, one could always resort to a telegram. The ominous yellow envelope held a flimsy sheet on which were affixed the printed strips of paper that had been conveyed via the telegraphy system. This was an expensive means of communication so the number of words used in a message was kept to a minimum. No room for embellishments – just a simple 'girl born today stop both well stop Harry stop' would be sufficient. On the whole, though, telegrams were greeted by most recipients with some trepidation, as they usually contained bad news. To start with they were not brought by the usual postman on his round, but came at any time of the day, hand delivered to a member of the household by the junior members of the Royal Mail service, who were distinguished by the smart pillbox hat which completed their navy blue uniform. The precious telegrams were carried in a small leather pouch fixed to a sturdy leather belt. The telegram delivery boy was much envied by his peers for not only had he been accepted into a steady career with prospects of advancement throughout the postal service, but he was equipped with a very distinctive red bicycle. He in turn was very conscious of the importance of his duties. He had to make sure that the telegram was actually delivered and read, usually on the doorstep, and had to be prepared to take down an answer to it, if required.

Where there was a telephone the imposing black instrument was usually placed in the hall, and in some places might even sport a cover to deter indiscriminate use.

The generation that reached maturity in the 1950s had grown up witnessing tremendous advances in scientific discoveries, culminating in 1946 with the indescribable horror of the atomic bomb. They had seen aircraft become more and more sophisticated and nuclear power then harnessed for peaceful purposes too; so much and so many were the dreams and visions of what the brave new world would hold. But if, in the 1950s, you had told a woman that one day she would carry her own personal telephone in her handbag, she would probably have laughed uncontrollably, so unlikely was that particular idea. For telephones, like refrigerators and cars, were really not for ordinary people. The wealthy, of course, were different. They had telephones so that they could contact tradesmen or chat to friends. Professional people like solicitors, doctors and dentists and those in certain businesses needed telephones for their work, but even they did not encourage the instrument to be used merely for social purposes. In the homes where there was a telephone the imposing black instrument was usually placed in the hall, and in some places might even sport a cover to deter indiscriminate use.

In rural areas, farmers who had been granted access to a telephone line during the war still had the even older models where the mouthpiece was attached to a piece of wood fixed to the wall and the receiver hung on a clip at the side. When you wished to make a call you depressed your receiver bar and when the operator in the local telephone exchange answered you asked her to connect you with whoever it was you required in the local area. So rare were the telephones in rural districts that the operators knew exactly which household was represented by which number. These were designated by the name of the village followed by two or possibly three digits. In some areas, each household had its own distinctive ring tone. In towns and cities, local calls could be dialled direct but anything outside the area required the assistance of the operator to connect you to 'the party you are calling', as it was expressed. It is odd to think now, in these days of automation, of all the large manned telephone exchanges that were in operation throughout the country, giving employment to thousands of – mainly female – telephonists. It is even stranger to recall that the telephone exchanges should have inspired a popular song as early as 1915 that enquired 'Which switch Miss, do I switch Miss, for Ipswich?' which conjures up a picture of all the plugs that confronted the telephonist in her work.

Although a home telephone was a rarity, it was important that everyone should have access to telephones and so public telephone boxes were installed at regular intervals. These iconic red boxes are fast disappearing from our landscape but still live on either in other countries where the British influence was strong in the past or as interesting relics in a theme park or in some mild eccentric's back garden. The kiosk was not large, it would take two adults at a pinch, but it offered privacy for your call. Inside there was a small mirror at eye height – most useful for checking one's make-up – and a notice that gave the 999 number for the emergency services. Beneath this was the heavy metal stand, which housed, on the left, the recess for holding the telephone directories and on the right another space suitable for holding one's handbag. In the centre, on the shelf below the little mirror, sat the telephone, and below that the boxes that received the money to pay for the call. These boxes contained slots into which were fed the pennies, sixpences and shillings needed to pay for the call. They also housed two press buttons marked A and B. To make a local call you placed two pennies in the slot and dialled the number you required. When the call was answered, button A was depressed and you were connected to whoever you were calling. Calls were timed to last for three minutes; seconds before this time was up, you would hear what were known as 'the pips'. This was a warning signal that either you should end the call or put a further two pennies in the box. If, however, there was no answer to your original call, you simply pressed button B and got your money back. Most children – and even some adults – had at some time or other entered a telephone box and pressed button B in the hope that the last user had failed to do so.

Should you have wished to make a trunk call – that is, one out of your immediate area – then the procedure was different. First it was necessary to come to the telephone box with an adequate supply of assorted coins. Next you lifted the receiver and dialled 0 for the operator to whom you gave the number you required. She would then tell you the cost of the initial call and once you had inserted that amount, she would place the call. If it was successful, again the pips would sound after three minutes and the operator would cut in to tell you how much more needed to be inserted in order to continue. It was often at this point that the occupant of the telephone box would open the door and enquire of anyone in the small queue that had formed if they had change for a two-shilling piece. One had to be very careful that in your generosity to help you didn't leave yourself short. Queues at the telephone box could be annoying, especially in cold weather, so it was not unknown to have irate people marching up and down, banging on the side of the box and pointing at their watches.

Every public telephone box had its own number, distinguished from a private line by the addition of an 'x'. During the days before their marriage it was possible for couples who lived a long distance from each other to make regular calls to one another by fixing a specific time, for example 8.30 p.m. every Thursday, having first established the numbers of their local box. The drawback to the system was if someone entered the box just before your allotted time. What could be quite unnerving, however, was if one just happened to be passing an empty telephone box when the telephone started to ring. Should one answer it or let it ring? There seemed to be no one hurrying to the spot. If one had a vivid imagination, you could invent a whole scenario around that missed call.

It was also considered important that children should know how to use a public telephone and to this end it became part of the training programme of every Girl Guide and Boy Scout. One never knew if a child might be required to make a call to the doctor in the event of serious illness in the home or, having spotted smoke issuing from an unexpected source, call the fire brigade, though there were also at that time special red-painted metal pillars at the roadside that housed an alarm directly connected to the fire station. These had a circular disc of toughened glass at the top, behind which was a handle. The instructions said one was to break the glass and pull the handle – but in the event of improper use there would be a penalty fine, so perhaps making a telephone call was less frightening.

By the end of the 1950s, the telephone had come within reach of more of the population, if there was availability in their area. The number of lines that the local exchange could offer was limited. In those days an actual line went from the main overhead telephone cables to be fixed to your house and in some cases only those for whom it was deemed really necessary would be allocated a telephone. Even if you were one of the chosen few, it might be that you had to share your line with a near neighbour. The main drawback to this was finding the other party engaged in conversation just at the moment when you wished to make a call. Of course, you promptly replaced your receiver, the click of which

163

would be heard by the other speakers, but then you could be left wondering if your own conversations were ever overheard. With the dawning of the 1960s, forward-thinking builders of new estates laid underground cables into the new houses, so you might become the proud possessor of a telephone connection even though you had no intention of taking on the commitment of a regular standing charge as well as the cost of each call. Besides which, why did we need a telephone? If we wanted to talk to friends and family, we either wrote them a letter or went to visit them. And if it was an emergency, well, there was always the public telephone box just round the corner.

While lamenting the demise of the letter, some might also regret the passing of the 'thank you' letter. D., in her wedding notebook, made sure that she noted down the date on which she received each wedding present, what it was and from whom it came. A tick beside each name indicates that she, like all brides at that time, promptly wrote a short letter to the sender saying how much their gift was appreciated. Her thank you would have been handwritten and would have actually named the gift so that the sender was in no doubt that it referred to what had been sent. In recent time 'busy' brides have resorted to the totally impersonal typed and then duplicated letters of thanks or bought cards baldly stating, 'Thank you for your kind gift'. This might be considered preferable to what is the worst scenario. You take time to select a gift from the list sent with your wedding invitation that costs more than you wanted to spend because it has to be purchased at one of the stockists chosen by the bride. If you attend the wedding reception, the bride may say a general rather than a personal thank you for the presents but the worst is when you have declined the invitation, sent your gift – and then heard nothing more. At least if your gift was a cheque you would see from your bank statement that it had been cashed, but as for the requested gift tokens or the expensive piece of china to match the dinner service – how are you to know if they ever reached their destination? In the 1950s this would have been considered as bad manners (as it still is for those of us who were brought up properly!). Many a Boxing Day was slightly marred for us as children as we were made to sit down and write our thank you letters, including the one to Aunt Maud thanking her for the ghastly purple jumper that was far too big, but we also learned to consider other people's feelings when our parents pointed out how many hours Aunt Maud had spent knitting the offending garment.

Nowadays, we are lucky if a grandchild makes a telephone call or sends a text message to acknowledge a gift. Yet we taught our children to write their thank you letters. So why has that part of life disappeared? When you stop and think about it, how often do you hear people, especially the young, actually use the words 'thank you'. Yet it is one of the very first words that one teaches a baby, or at least it used to be. At a recent award ceremony, a group of children took it in turns to receive a certificate and shake hands with the guest of honour. Most of them managed the handshake but very few indeed uttered the magic words as they took their certificate. From all of this can we deduce that good manners, as we knew them, no longer exist?

If it was an emergency, well, there was always the public telephone box just round the corner.

In the early 1950s the focal point of the living room was the hearth. In those pre-centrally heated houses, the living room was often the only room in the house that was heated. On a cold winter's evening there was nothing more pleasing than to come home to the warmth of a coal fire. Never mind that someone had had to clean out the remnants of the previous day's fire, trying to avoid sending the dust from the ashes all over the room. If the family were out all day, it was usual for the housewife to clear the hearth either before or immediately after breakfast, so she would have time to lay the new one and dust the room too before she went off to work. The fire was usually made with scrunched-up newspaper overlaid with thin sticks of wood known as kindling. Any large pieces of cinder from the previous night's fire might be placed on top, interspersed with small pieces of coal. The debris from the previous day was swept into a pan and taken outside, either to be thrown on any unmade garden paths or into the galvanised dustbin, which every house had. The coal scuttle was filled and put beside the hearth, which was usually tiled and was bounded by a fender. If there were young children in the house then a fireguard was essential to keep them away from falling into the fire. Some coal at that time had a habit of 'spitting' and throwing out a jet of flame from the grate; there was also an additional danger from coals suddenly shifting and projecting a glowing ember which, if there were no fender, could land on the hearthrug or carpet and start another fire. A very dangerous habit that still existed in the 1950s was that of placing a looking glass or mirror above the mantelpiece. It was rumoured that many young girls were known to have stood on the fender to look in the mirror and in doing so were severely burned when their dresses caught fire.

However, there was nothing quite like the family gathered round the fireside, toasting their toes and burning their legs while the back of them felt the draughts that came in from single-glazed, perhaps ill-fitting windows or under the door that led from the hall. The answer was often to build the fire bigger or start it off earlier in the day in order to get the room thoroughly warmed. Coal was much in demand for all the new houses that were being built, as well as all the ones already in existence, and they had to be provided with brick-built coal bunkers. In addition to keeping the home fires burning, Britain's factories were burning coal at a tremendous rate to power the machines to produce the goods that would make the country a competitive market, as well as providing all the consumer goods Brits would one day buy. Coal also powered the trains and many British ships, as well as producing the gas and electricity that was used in homes and factories. Coal was everywhere. And burning coal was not just producing heat, it was belching out thick black smoke into the air and depositing soot on to everything with which it came into contact. No one then spoke of damaging the ozone layer – in those days ozone was the bracing air one encountered at the seaside – but everyone was aware that there were health dangers related to breathing in the sooty air, particularly in wintertime when bronchitis was rife in industrial areas. The London pea-soup fogs that feature so strongly in Victorian novels became known as 'smog' in the 1950s. In 1952 London was brought to a standstill for four days when it was shrouded in a dense mix of smoke and fog (something that has been seen since in Japan and China). In London, the noxious mixture of gases is said to have been responsible for 4,000 deaths in those four days alone.

Over the next few months the death toll attributed to smog-related pulmonary diseases was put at twice that number. The result was that government action finally brought in the Clean Air Act in 1956 that permitted only the use of smokeless fuel such as Coalite. This did not eradicate smog entirely but the ensuing fogs were less damaging than before.

What the Clean Air Act did do was to change designers' thoughts about the place of the hearth in the home. Already the advent of the television set in the home had tended to change the configuration of the living room. At first gas or electric fires were set into the recess occupied by the grate. Then houses were built without a chimney and traditional fireplace, with electric heaters inset into a wall. Once central heating had arrived the old-fashioned fireplace was very definitely a thing of the past. Victorian and Edwardian black-leaded grates, often with their accompanying hand-painted tiles, were ripped out and sent off to the scrapyard. But later, wood-burning stoves reminded people that they did like to see a glowing fire and slowly, slowly, those living in houses with chimneys have reinstated their fireplaces and occasionally they might buy a bag of smokeless fuel and have a 'real fire'. But their children will never be deputed by mother to count in the sacks of coal carried by the begrimed coalman from the lorry parked outside in the street down the passage at the side of the house to the coal shed down the garden. Each sack contained a hundredweight of coal and if mother had ordered a ton then the child, remembering their tables, would solemnly count the twenty sacks as they passed the window. If you lived in a house with a coal cellar, there was the excitement of watching the circular metal lid in the pavement close to the front door being lifted and the coalman emptying the sacks into the cellar below with a great crash and a rumble as the shiny black lumps cascaded downwards.

Similarly, the modern child is unfamiliar with the sweep, who used to call at the end of winter to clean the chimney. For the housewife this visit entailed quite a bit of preparation. To start with the sweep always announced he would arrive early so arrangements had to be made to get breakfast over and done with before he came. Then furniture had to be covered in dust sheets, and the curtains taken down ready to be washed along with anything else in the room, such as the glass light shade that might pick up a coating of soot. If it was a fine day the hearthrug would be taken outside to hang on the washing line, ready to be given a good beating before going back to its place, and old sheets were put down to cover the carpet or linoleum entirely. If all this seems excessive, one has to bear in mind that the sweep himself wore clothes that were covered with soot and that once the sweeping operation began there was no knowing what might happen. In the 1950s the sweep would present himself at the back door, never the front, as that would have meant carrying soot through the house. He would leave his handcart outside in the road, for in those days he probably lived near enough to all his regular customers to be able to push his cart to them, though some sweeps did use pedal-driven carts. With his grimy bag of tools at his side, having first assessed the height of the chimney, he would connect the circular brush to a pole and introduce it into the chimney, slowly connecting pole to pole until he had the required length. At this point he might well engage the services of the children of the house to run outside to see if the brush had arrived above the chimneypot. Once this stage had been reached it was the tricky stage of bringing the brush down again, gently sweeping the soot down with it rather than it coming down in a whoosh that would cover everything at floor level. At the end of the process, the sweep departed, either taking with him all the soot from your chimney or leaving it outside for you to spread later on your celery plants or roses. Nothing was wasted in those days!

The sweep departed ... taking with him all the soot from your chimney or leaving it outside for you to spread later on your celery plants or roses.

From smog to chimney soot, we move to smoking. We have already mentioned how widespread cigarette smoking was in the 1950s and we have all noted in recent years the attempts to prevent the habit and the legislation that has imposed bans on smoking in public places. It is hard now to remember that in the 1950s not only did we inhale smoke as we sat in the cinema, but it was also common practice for smokers to light up between courses in restaurants or to linger with a cigar over coffee and a brandy at the end of a meal, totally regardless of those around them who might be eating. Cigarettes are still sold, mainly in newsagents' shops, but most of the specialist tobacconists of the 1950s have long since disappeared. Most towns had several of these scattered around the central area as well as in the roads leading off it. Each shop had a narrow frontage of a single window that housed, amongst other items, a display of pipes, for pipe smoking was also very popular in the 1950s not only with older men but with young men too, who fancied that it was suave to do so. Many of the models used in knitting patterns for men's jumpers and pullovers at that time featured a good-looking young man either holding a pipe at a jaunty angle or posing with a pipe clenched between his perfect teeth. Along with the pipes of various types and those made by leading manufacturers, a child could be tempted inside the shop to purchase a clay pipe with which to blow bubbles. That was in the days before you could buy small tins of liquid containing detergent and a small hoop of wire, which was dabbled in the liquid prior to being blown to form bubbles – fun but not half so satisfying as blowing soapy water through a clay pipe, providing you remembered not to breathe in when you should have been blowing!

Inside the tobacconist's, one side of the narrow shop was occupied with the counter and the display cases that housed everything that was smoking related. There, one had no problem finding Christmas and birthday presents for men of every age group: silver cigarette cases, onyx ash trays and cigarette boxes, pipe racks, lighters in all shapes and sizes right down to cigarette papers and loose tobacco with names like Digger Mixture and Shag. (Another word that has changed its meaning!) Our 1950s housewife would no doubt have visited such shops, if not for herself then for the men in her family. Also should she suddenly have need for a walking stick then the tobacconist's was the place to find it – a cylindrical holder full of plain wooden walking sticks with curved handles always stood just inside the door. While, just outside the door of some tobacconists, would stand a huge model figure of either a kilted Scotsman or a stereotypical Native American. Presumably the specialist tobacconist ceased to be able to make a living when cigarette vending machines appeared in pubs and restaurants, as well as when cigarettes began to be sold at supermarkets.

In a similar way the ironmongery stores, which sold tools of all shapes, sizes and purposes as well as things like nails, tacks and screws, not in small packets but by the ounce or even individually, have been replaced by the large DIY stores. Nothing is more frustrating than finding when one needs say, seven cup hooks, that they are now sold only in packets of six, thus causing the customer to buy two packets just to get the extra one. Those shops of the past always stocked the most unusual things, often tucked away in a cardboard box in a drawer: a washer to fit an old tap, a small scrap of leather that was exactly what you needed for a repair, even a replacement mantle for a gaslight. The list is endless. In the 1950s we still repaired things, shoes amongst them. Again, everywhere had a shoe repairer, whether it was a one-man enterprise in a shed in a village or a larger operation in town. People were still wearing shoes with leather soles and heels and as they wore out, they would take them to the shop to be repaired. The smaller shops operated their machinery in full view of the public and often one would have to wait until the repairer had finished a certain operation before he would switch off the machine so that you could hear each other. The shop had its own special smell of heated leather and if one had nothing better to do then it was interesting to watch as a new sole was put in place or tips were placed on a pair of high heels. The introduction of synthetic materials and shoes that did not need repairing spelt the slow decline for the shoe repairer. In time, he was forced to diversify into offering a key-cutting service and engraving cups and medals.

With the loss of the shoe repairer we lost a commodity known as heel ball. This came in sticks in either black or brown and was used to seal the edges of the leather that was used in a repair. Once the repairer had ceased trading it was difficult for the man who still repaired his family's shoes to get hold of both leather and heel ball. Another use of the latter was for artistic purposes. During the 1950s there was an awakened interest in the history that was to be found in our parish churches and so people visited them armed with large sheets of paper of the type used by fried fish shops to wrap their wares and a stick of black heel ball in order to make rubbings of the brass memorials of the past. The demise of heel ball proved to be a blessing in saving the surface of the brass.

It is tempting to lament the passing of many of the good things from the 1950s but we must not, we are told, stand in the way of progress. Nonetheless, those from the 1950s may feel strongly that in our search for equality we have failed to raise standards and, at the risk of sounding like grumpy old women, we forward-looking 1950s girls despair at the changes to the English language. We may not hanker for the return of the clipped vowel sounds that emanated from the film studios of Elstree and Pinewood, but at least we could understand what was being said. Where once actors and actresses, as well as those aspiring to promotion in their professions, took care to enunciate carefully and possibly even erased regional accents in an effort not to betray their class background, the pendulum seems to have swung so far the other way that it is no longer possible to identify either class or nationality, for that matter, through speech. We have also seen the use and misuse of language in contexts unknown in the 1950s. Not only have well-loved adjectives taken on a new meaning, some have been turned into nouns. The growth in technology has given us a whole new vocabulary, as has the huge expansion of governmental influence in all aspects of our lives, not least in introducing us to lengthy forms that have mangled English grammar as we knew it. There are occasions when one is reminded forcibly of the 'newspeak' of George Orwell's *1984*. But, however much the 1950s housewife may look back to the early days of her marriage, she has to admit that there were hard times and that she would not be enjoying her retirement now if it was not for the good times that came in between.

15

Let's Talk About Sex

Those who are in the habit of picking up a book and reading the last chapter first may be somewhat taken aback by the rather blunt heading to this chapter, for sex was one subject that was rarely mentioned in polite company. It was almost as if it did not exist. There was a joke in the 1950s that was partly a criticism of the affected speech of certain parts of society at the time who would insist on pronouncing 'a' as 'e', that ran along the lines that 'sex is what the poor people have their coal delivered in!'

It had always been accepted that the upper classes had quite different standards to the other classes. Everyone had either met or read about someone who was the illegitimate offspring of a poor misused servant girl and the 'lord of the manor', but they didn't talk about that anymore than they talked about 'mistakes' that may have happened in their own families, especially in wartime. On the whole, the majority of the nation regarded 'making love' or sexual intercourse as something to be conducted in the privacy, and possibly darkness, of one's bedroom and therefore of no concern to anyone else. The word 'intercourse' often appeared in reports of notable divorce cases in Sunday newspapers such as the *News of the World*. Any intelligent child who avidly read whatever was available and used a dictionary too was likely to grin during school assembly when confronted with the hymn that spoke of a 'closer intercourse with Him'. Ironically, in this free, liberated twenty-first century we still use the euphemistic phrase, 'sleeping together' even though practically every primary school child is well aware that sleeping is not the main activity involved.

This is not the place to delve into either the religious influences or the deep-seated psychological reasons why parents in the past were so reluctant to talk to their children about procreation. Suffice it to say that in the 1950s most girls had gained what they knew about sex from their schoolfellows; quite where they got theirs from was never made clear. Some girls' schools, however, actually tackled the vital question of how a baby was made by dealing with it in a biology lesson:

We knew from the girls in the year above that when we got to the Rabbit lesson, all would be revealed. When the day came we had a young biology teacher who was due to marry at the end of term, so that made it all the more exciting. We spent part of the lesson drawing the cross section of the rabbit's interior organs in our notebooks and labelling different parts of its anatomy. But it was getting close to the end of the lesson and we still hadn't got to the part we were waiting for. Finally, a very pink Miss explained the copulation of rabbits. The bell rang for the end of the lesson. She picked up her books and made for the lab door, turned and said 'And the same thing applies to human beings!' And that was all the sex education we had in our Grammar School!

I'd had very little to do with boys. When I went off to University in 1952, my older, married sister took me to one side and gave me a present of a book of stamps and said, 'if you get into trouble, promise me you won't do anything silly'. Although I hadn't a clue what she was getting at, both of us were too embarrassed either to say more or to ask questions.

My sister, who was a student nurse, showed me a book called *The Wonderful Story of the Human Body*. This had diagrams of the male and female body and even depicted a foetus in the womb. It was all very clinical but I still had no idea how 'mating' was achieved.

Even those who knew all the facts were not always prepared for the strong emotions that physical love could arouse both in themselves and their partner. As we said earlier many girls started their married lives entirely unprepared for what lay ahead of them on their wedding night. Over and over again contributors told of their ignorance and of the fact that their mothers failed to give them any advice or guidance, merely hinting with some embarrassment at what might happen; sometimes suggesting, perhaps as a result of their own experience, that it would be a painful experience that had to be endured. Other mothers – and occasionally mothers-in-law – would casually leave a book or a leaflet in a bedside drawer that contained helpful information in preparation for the wedding night:

A visit to the barber's shop by a young man might elicit the discreet enquiry as he paid for his haircut, 'do you require anything for the weekend, Sir?

> The week before we married my future mother-in-law gave me a small leaflet to take home with me. Among the items headed 'what to do on your wedding night' it described how you were bound to be very tired after a long and exciting day. Therefore, the writer advised, that when you had both prepared yourselves for bed, you should kneel down together beside the bed and pray. Once you had both given thanks for being brought together, you would feel Divine blessing and peace and be able to fall gently to sleep – leaving other things for another day!
>
> I knew nothing about the intimate side of marriage. My mother told me nothing. She did say my new husband would tell me, as he had been in the navy.

At least the bride-to-be whose mother gave her a copy of Marie Stopes' book *Married Love* to read had more practical guidance to help her.

Despite their lack of knowledge and experience most contributors reported that they quickly settled into a satisfying sex life with their husbands. Time and time again they reported how gentle and supportive their husbands had been. Initially, once a couple had decided that either for financial or housing reasons they did not wish to start a family immediately, it was the husband who took the necessary precautions to prevent conception. In this age of sexual liberation it is difficult to comprehend what it was like in the

1950s when contraception was acknowledged but not encouraged, certainly not by some branches of the Church. Contraceptives came in the form of condoms, then mostly called by their nicknames of French letters or rubber johnnies, or simply by the trade name of Durex. These were not on display anywhere. A visit to the barber's shop by a young man might elicit the discreet enquiry as he paid for his haircut, 'do you require anything for the weekend, Sir?' If the answer was in the affirmative, then the little packets were produced. Otherwise the only other supplier was the chemist. Again, the man couldn't just select what he wanted and pay for it – he had to ask! The items would then be produced from under the counter, almost like a black market packet of biscuits. It took courage for a young man, even though now married, to ask a female assistant in the chemist's shop for what he wanted and often he would hang around staring into glass display cabinets until he could approach the male chemist.

Condoms were not 100 per cent reliable and perhaps, after the scare of an unwanted pregnancy or where it was decided that a family must definitely be postponed, the woman took responsibility for contraception. Generations before the 'morning-after pill' was created, women had taken steps to make sure that the coital act did not result in pregnancy by using douches or sponges soaked in whatever was considered at the time as being the best mixture to act as an anti-spermicidal agent. Right up to the late 1940s many women were also using Rendells suppositories, which consisted of a mixture of quinine and cocoa-nut butter.

The Family Planning Association (FPA) dated back to the 1930s when five different groups amalgamated with the express aim 'that married people may space or limit their families and thus might mitigate the evils of ill health and poverty'. This was a worrying social problem: too many extra-large families needed handouts from the Poor Law Guardians, overcrowded housing led to neglect and the spread of disease, while producing a child almost annually often led to the severe breakdown in the health of thousands of women. Add to them all those who died in childbirth or from botched backstreet abortions and the country was presented with caring for all the orphaned families who had to be taken into the workhouse or children's homes.

The FPA offered advice to married women who were then mainly fitted with the internal device known as the diaphragm or Dutch cap. However, right up to the end of the 1940s the services of the FPA were available only to married couples. Then, in 1950, a concession was made for couples about to marry. To receive help before the actual wedding day, the bride-to-be had to turn up at one of the FPA clinics armed with a letter from either her doctor or the officiating vicar to verify that she really was about to become a married woman. Later during the 1950s, trials were begun on the contraceptive pill but even when the pill went into production it was, of course, only available on prescription from the doctor – for married women. The so-called age of sexual liberation had still to dawn.

The 1950s couples who had strong religious beliefs practised what was known as the rhythm method or natural contraception, which entailed knowing exactly at what stage of the woman's menstrual cycle she was likely to be less fertile and therefore when it was 'safe' to have intercourse. For the couple trying to have a baby, this method worked in reverse, intercourse taking place when the woman was most fertile.

Most of the contributors to this work had babies within the first year to eighteen months of their marriage, which suggests that they had been reluctant to seek outside advice on contraception. Overall, most couples had their first child within three years, even those who had delayed starting a family because they were in one of the professions such as teaching or nursing where they were expected to continue with their careers, or they needed to work in order to help support their husbands who were studying to increase their own career prospects. Once the financial situation improved and a settled home was secured, the nesting instinct took hold and then the 1950s housewife prepared for the next big challenge in her life, that of becoming a mother and bringing up a baby in the 1950s.

Sources

The Festival of Britain Guide.

Practical Cookery for All (Odhams Press, 1953 – illustrations taken from the book).

Good Housekeeping's Popular Cookery (The National Magazine Company, 1949).

Woman's Weekly, April 1959.

Stitchcraft, July 1950, July 1951–January 1959.

Colin Raistrick, archivist of Proctor & Gamble. (Advertisements for Tampax reproduced by kind permission of Proctor & Gamble.)

'Divorce in England, 1950–2000: A Moral Tale'. Paper by Carol Smart, 29 October 1990.
Chapter 13 quotation from the Royal Commission on Marriage and Divorce, 1956.

'The Story of a Supermarket' – the Sainsbury's Archive at the Museum of London website.

'Utility Furniture and Household Furnishings' – Board of Trade Leaflet UFD/6.

A wedding notebook of furniture, presents, etc., 1956 (unpublished).

Appendices

Popular Books of the 1950s

Achebe, Chinua, *Things Fall Apart*
Amis, Kingsley, *Lucky Jim*
Baldwin, James, *Go Tell it on the Mountain*
Beckett, Samuel, *The Beckett Trilogy*
Burroughs, William, *Naked Lunch*
Chandler, Raymond, *The Long Goodbye*
Christie, Agatha, *A Murder is Announced*
Compton-Burnett, Ivy, *A Heritage and Its History*
du Maurier, Daphne, *My Cousin Rachel*
Ellison, Ralph, *The Invisible Man*
Frame, Janet, *Owls Do Cry*
Golding, William, *The Lord of the Flies*
Hartley, L.P., *The Go-Between*
Hemingway, Ernest, *The Old Man and the Sea*
Heyer, Georgette, *The Grand Sophyie*
Heyerdahl, Thor, *The Kon-Tiki Expedition*
Highsmith, Patricia, *The Talented Mr Ripley*
Jenkins, Elizabeth, *The Tortoise and the Hare*
Kerouac, Jack, *On the Road*
Lehmann, Rosamond, *The Echoing Grove*
Macaulay, Rose, *The Towers of Trebizond*
McCullers, Carson, *The Ballad of the Sad Café*
Nabokov, Vladimir, *Lolita*
Powell, Anthony, *A Dance to the Music of Time*
Salinger, J.D., *The Catcher in the Rye*
Sillitoe, Alan, *Saturday Night and Sunday Morning*

Steinbeck, John, *East of Eden*
Taylor, Elizabeth, *Angel*
Townsend Warner, Sylvia, *The Flint Anchor*
Waugh, Evelyn, *The Sword of Honour* trilogy
West, Rebecca, *The Fountain Overflows*
Wyndham, John, *The Chrysalids*
Wyndham, John, *The Day of the Triffids*
Wyndham, John, *The Kraken Wakes*
Wyndham, John, *The Midwich Cuckoos*

Popular Radio Programmes of the 1950s

The BBC provided two main outlets for its programmes. The Home Service specialised mainly in speech-based talks and lectures of the more serious kind and was responsible for the delivery of regular news broadcasts, comment and educational programmes, as well as providing high-quality drama. The Home Service also took care of the religious needs of the nation, broadcasting the Daily Service each weekday morning, sometimes relayed from a church rather than from the studio. In retrospect, the BBC was definitely ahead of its time, for occasionally the whole service would be taken by a woman, usually one who had been ordained in one of the Nonconformist denominations. Religious services were also broadcast every Sunday and on all the major festivals throughout the year. The Home Service also provided children with an hour of their very own at five o'clock each weekday evening. The programmes were very varied but are now remembered by listeners from the 1950s as providing them with, among other things, wonderful adaptations of books and plays.

The Third Programme, which was introduced much later, was aimed at smaller audiences, mainly lovers of classical music. Air time was restricted to evenings only.

The Light Programme, as its name implies, was responsible for both light music programmes, as opposed to classical, and light entertainment, that is – situation comedies and sketch shows – usually lasting half an hour. This was the era when many great writing talents flourished, who helped turn individual artistes into celebrities. The lists below are not comprehensive but contain the most mentioned (and loved) programmes.

Music
Family Favourites
Friday Night is Music Night
Grand Hotel – (The Palm Court Orchestra)
Henry Hall's Guest Night
Housewives' Choice

The Billy Cotton Band Show
Variety Bandbox

The commercial station Radio Luxembourg also provided music throughout the evenings, particularly the *Top Twenty*, while the Home Service had a daily lunchtime concert of classical music.

Comedy Programmes

Many of these had been popular in the 1940s and continued in various forms into the 1960s.

Beyond Our Ken
Educating Archie
Hancock's Half Hour
Life with the Lyons
Meet the Huggetts
Much-Binding-in-the-Marsh
PC 49
Ray's a Laugh
Round the Horne
Take it From Here
The Al Read Show
The Clitheroe Kid
The Goon Show – this seems to have been the nation's favourite
The Navy Lark

Other Favourites

Desert Island Discs
Down Your Way – an attempt to take radio out of the studio and to the people. Each week there was a different location and local people were interviewed in an effort to create a sound picture of the area
Gardeners' Question Time
Have a Go – Yorkshireman Wilfred Pickles and his wife Mabel toured small towns and villages throughout the country, offering contestants the chance to win very small sums of money in a quiz show. For some time the musical accompaniment at the piano was provided by Violet Carson, aka Auntie Vi on *Children's Hour*. When television started she found a new career as Ena Sharples in *Coronation Street*.
In Town Tonight
Journey Into Space
Letter from America
Mrs Dale's Diary
The Adventures of Paul Temple
The Archers

Appointment with Fear – this was one to listen to in the dark and scare yourself silly. Valentine Dyall's voice, *The Man in Black*, sent shivers down your spine as he narrated eerie stories
Twenty Questions
Woman's Hour

Popular Television Shows of the 1950s

Most contributors barely mentioned television programmes, mainly due to the fact that not many people had sets or were able to receive television signals in their area.

The only programmes mentioned were:

Wagon Train
What's My Line?
Whirligig
Muffin the Mule

Popular Plays of the 1950s

A Long Day's Journey into Night
A Taste of Honey
A View from the Bridge
Becket
Chicken Soup with Barley
The End Game
Epitaph for George Dillon
I Am a Camera
Inherit the Wind
Look Back in Anger
My Fair Lady
Relative Values
Ring Round the Moon
Romanoff and Juliet
Sabrina Fair
Separate Tables
Serjeant Musgrave's Dance
Suddenly, Last Summer
Summer of the Seventeenth Doll
Tea and Sympathy
The Birthday Party
The Chalk Garden
The Cocktail Party
The Crucible
The Dark is Light Enough

The Deep Blue Sea
The Dumb Waiter
The Entertainer
The House by the Lake
The Long and the Short and the Tall
The Miracle Worker
The Mousetrap
The Potting Shed
The Reluctant Debutante
The Rose Tattoo
The Sleeping Prince
The Tea House of the August Moon
Waiting for Godot
Waltz of the Toreadors

Popular Musicals of the 1950s

Call Me Madam
Can-Can
Damn Yankees
Free As Air
Gay's the Word
Guys and Dolls
Gypsy
Kismet
La Plume de Ma Tante
Lock Up Your Daughters
Salad Days
The Boy Friend
The Sound of Music
Valmouth
Wish You Were Here

Revues and entertainments
Cambridge Footlights
Flanders and Swann

Popular Films of the 1950s

A Night to Remember
A Street Car Named Desire
All About Eve
An Affair to Remember
An American in Paris

Animal Farm
Annie Get Your Gun
Arms and the Man
Around the World in Eighty Days
Bell, Book and Candle
Bonjour Tristesse
Carmen Jones
Cat on a Hot Tin Roof
Chance of a Lifetime
Cyrano de Bergerac
Dial M for Murder
East of Eden
Expresso Bongo
From Here to Eternity
Funny Face
Gentlemen Prefer Blondes
Gigi
Gone to Earth
Guys and Dolls
Hans Christian Andersoen
High Noon
High Society
I'm All Right Jack
Ice Cold in Alex
Julius Caesar
La Strada
The Lady and the Tramp
Laughter in Paradise
Lilli Marlene
Love Is a Many-Splendid Thing
Mandy
Odette
Oklahoma!
Paths of Glory
Quatermass 2
Rear Window
Reluctant Heroes
Richard III
Roman Holiday
Sabrina
Separate Tables
Seven Brides for Seven Brothers
Shane
Singin' in the Rain
So Long at the Fair
Some Like it Hot

South Pacific
The African Queen
The Blue Lamp
The Browning Version
The Caine Mutiny
The Colditz Story
The Dambusters
The Dancing Years
The Day the Earth Stood Still
The Great Escape
The Happiest Days of Your Life
The Horse's Mouth
The Inn of the Sixth Happiness
The King and I
The Lavender Hill Mob
The Magic Box
The Matchmaker
The Moulin Rouge
The Nun's Story
The Old Man and the Sea
The Pajama Game
The Quatermass Xperiment
The Reluctant Debutante
The Robe
The Seven Year Itch
The Small Miracle
The Snows of Kilimanjaro
The Tales of Hoffman
The Teahouse of the August Moon
The Wooden Horse
To Catch a Thief

'And many more', as the advertisements for songs on a record used to say.

Popular Advertisements of the 1950s

Had it been possible to reproduce some of the advertisements popular in the 1950s, we would have been able to see how dated some of them seem while others appear to have changed very little in getting their message across. Unfortunately copyright restrictions prevent this, so a list of products is given instead. The following all appeared in the brochure of the Festival of Britain in 1951. The advertisements varied in size but all were colourful. This is the order in which they appeared:

Benedict Processed Peas
Ovaltine
BOAC/BEA

Heinz 57
Hoover – washing machine and vacuum cleaner
Crompton Lamps (electric light bulbs)
Prestige – kitchenware
Manfield – shoes
Carr's of Carlisle Biscuits
Macleans Toothpaste
Number Seven – Abdulla 'Virginia' cigarettes; twenty for 3s 10d
Kayser Bondor – stockings and lingerie
Cow & Gate Ltd – baby food
'His Master's Voice' – television, radio, records
Cussons Imperial Leather – soap, talcum powder and other toilet luxuries
Carter-Horseley (Engineers) Ltd
Cossor – electronics
EMI – the electronic heart of Britain
The Standard Vanguard – Standard, Triumph, commercial vehicles, Ferguson tractors
Lloyds Bank Ltd
Allied Ironfounders Ltd
Addis – Britain's biggest name in brushes
Curtis Gin – 'those who know … know Curtis Gin the world over'
EKCO – radio and television
Dunlop – leaders of progress in rubber
Costain Ltd – building and civil engineering contractors
Shell-Mex and BP
Black & White Scotch Whisky
Rootes Group Products
Ford of Dagenham
Capstan Navy Cut Cigarettes
The English Electric Co. Ltd
Ronson Cigarette Lighters
Marconi – radio, radar and television
State Express 555 – cigarettes
Napier – air and marine internal combustion engineers
Wolsey – nylons
Outspan – oranges and grapefruit from South Africa
Creda and Simplex – electric cookers, water heaters, kettles, irons and electric fires
Ingersoll – 10-lever locks
Craven A – cigarettes
Horlicks
Siemens – electric lamps and supplies
TI Light Engineering
Coalite Smokeless Coal
Mr Therm – 'Gas at your service'
Sanderson – wallpapers and fabrics

Sperry – precision navigation equipment
Edward Sharp & Sons Ltd – the toffee specialists
VAT 69 – Scotch whisky
Girling – brakes
National Benzole Co. Ltd – Mr Mercury
Haig – whisky

Although there is no mention of 'wild, wild women', one could be forgiven, when reading this list, of thinking of the song that mentions cigarettes and whisky as well, for there seem to be more advertisements for those two items than any other. It should be remembered, however, that the Festival of Britain was aimed at buyers from other countries with whom Britain hoped to establish trading links. At that time Britain had large tobacco-processing factories throughout the country, which employed a huge workforce. Similarly, the Scottish distilleries relied on increasing their export trade. What is interesting about the cigarette advertisements included here is that they all portray smoking as being sophisticated. One shows an elegant woman in evening dress while another depicts a couple at the races. The cigarettes shown were expensive, high-quality brands, certainly not the Woodbines of the working man.

Magazines and newspapers also carried advertisements. These varied from full- and half-size pages, down to small boxes within a column that related to everyday problems, often of a medical nature. For example, the back cover of a 1959 women's magazine was entirely given over to Jeyes' Hygienic Toilet Tissue. The blurb describes it as being 'soft, yet not over-soft, not *too* absorbent – and therefore safe for all the family'. For a generation brought up, often, on cut-up squares of newspaper or harsh, shiny lavatory paper, this was an advance but nowhere near the softness one expects nowadays from the item. The advertisement also reminds one of how popular the porcelain paper holders were in some bathrooms. These came in white, black and 'six contemporary colours, smart, modern, neat and tidy'. A box of interfolded sheets to fit a holder cost 1*s* 3*d* but for everyday family use a roll of 500 sheets was only 1*s* 2*d*.

Below is a random selection of advertisements aimed at women in the first half of the 1950s:

Aertex underwear
Amami Wave Set
Anadin, Phensic
Arrid Deodorant
Bristow's Lanolin Shampoo – 'avoid parched hair this summer'
Cuticura Soap and Hand Cream
Fleet Foot – sports shoes
Flexcello – expanding rib top stockings, rayon, all wool, lisle lined
Freezone Liquid Corn Remover

Liberty Shoes Ltd, Leicester
Lucozade
Lux Soap and Soap Flakes
Marmola anti-fat tablets
Ovaltine – promoted as a refreshing cold summer drink
Pond's Cold Cream
Silcott Sanitary towels
Tampax

Another mixed bag from a 1959 women's magazine:

Bonio – for the dog
Calsalettes – vegetable-based laxatives
Darkaline High Gloss Stain
Doan's Backache and Kidney Pills
English Rose Foundation Garments
Flowerdell's Tablets for Threadworm
Iron-Ox – tablets to improve the blood
Japlac – one-coat lacquer to transform the house
John Nobles Catalogue
Knight's Castile Soap
Lavendo – silicone wax furniture polish
Oat Krunchies – a new cereal from Quaker
Omo Washing Powder
PLJ – lemon juice, a long promotion that ends, for a 'lithe outline, jewel-clear skin … no more natural beauty aid'
Portland – shoes
Sanatogen Tonic Wine
Shadeine – treatment to hide greying hair
Socumfi – shoes for the whole family
Vedona – underwear

From this list it would be easy to assume that 1950s women were concerned about their health and keeping a slim figure, with or without the aid of foundation garments. Also, that they tried to keep encroaching age at bay and took pride in keeping their homes spick and span. In all, were they very different from today's women?

Index